Dancing with Divorce

Dancing with Divorce

Ted K. Lodewijks

Concrescent Letters

Dancing with Divorce © 2016 Ted K. Lodewijks

All rights reserved. Except for brief quotations in a review, the book, or parts thereof, may not be reproduced in any work without permission in writing from the publisher. The moral rights of the author have been asserted.

The right of Ted K. Lodewijks to be identified as the author of this work has been asserted by them in accordance with the Copyright, Designs and Patents Act, 1988.

For information contact:
Concrescent Letters, an imprint of Concrescent LLC
Richmond CA, USA
info@Concrescent.net

ISBN: 978-0-9903927-4-3

Library of Congress Control Number: 2016934301

Within...

Welcome
11

In the Beginning...
13

Lesotho Nights
109

Depression
161

Kids & Divorce
189

The Dating Game
217

Where am I now?
245

Welcome

If I had to look back at the past 6 years and attempt to recall what happened, what went wrong and how it managed to work itself out, I would not believe it all possible.

I had been married to the girl of my dreams for 19 years, we had 2 beautiful daughters and despite the daily challenges life sprinkled on our lives, it seemed groovy. We had a lovely home, three dogs and a lemon tree. Then it seemed as if someone removed the steering wheel, cut the brake line and pushed the vehicle down a steep hill.

This is collection of memories taken from my perspective and expressed as I encountered and interpreted them at that precise moment. The highs and lows, anger and joy and harsh reality of the many faces of divorce were largely captured on a Blackberry for the first year typed in the early hours of the morning as I searched for sleep. It eluded me and sent instead its hairy inbred cousins, fear and panic.

I was divorced at the age of 44 and with my worldly possessions packed into a Fiat Uno, I left uncertain of what adventures I would encounter and where I was going. I was not gung ho Captain America racing into the battlefield, but more like Scooby Doo petrified to glance around the corner or open a cupboard door. I had nowhere to go and as I drove out of our front gate, I wept as I glanced in my rear view mirror and saw my wife, two daughters and my dog watching me.

It is a journey into myself and dealing with demons I did not want to face, confronting reality when I was not able to and accepting assistance despite my pride. Friendships for life were forged and old friendships seemed to fade, people chose sides and it was difficult, but understandable.

The purpose of this book is not to point fingers and shift blame, it is neither the attempt to glorify my journey through all of this and not intended to be a DIY Divorce Kit Made Easy. Rather, it was a coping mechanism suggested to assist in my recovery by my therapist. By coping I mean surviving, not similar to that feeling one encounters after disposing of a trifle made for 6 with the aid of a silver spoon and excitement of a teenage boy braving his first shave.

Am I surprised I am still alive, that I survived to tell the tale? That I live another day to embrace, chase and pace through another day? Indeed I am. This I can only attribute to a loving Mom who still to this day loves me more than a teacher loves school holidays, or a bean convention promoter loves air freshener. Good friends who stood up and offered more than they ever needed to and fed and comforted me when I was no longer able to care for myself.

I never expected to be where I am today and as I reflect on the years that have passed and the darkness that cloaked my life, it is more than I ever hoped for and more. So be encouraged, be alarmed, grab a carrot, cow sandwich, cup of tea or mug of coffee and turn the page, I dare you.

In the Beginning...

This is the terror of divorce and loss, this is the monster that I had to face and the pages that follow are an indication of the hell I went through over a 3 month period. I questioned my faith, my self-worth, life and came the closest I had ever come to taking my own life.

It was a continual flow of raw emotions and questions and pleas for help and forgiveness in a world I no longer understood or wanted to be a part of.

The despair, tears and desperate search are real as are the love and support I received from friends and family.

So the Truth,

All has not been well, I cry a lot, I have to force myself to eat (yes this is Ted) and I miss my girls terribly. I had them for the weekend and when I dropped them at school this morning, I could not look them in the eye when saying goodbye for fear of breaking down in front of them.

Am I doing anything about it, yes, I am trying to be honest with friends about my true state of being instead of joking all the time. This goes completely against my coping mechanisms and I am in a completely unfamiliar ground.

I started taking St Johns Wort today in an attempt to make myself more pleasant naturally, I contacted a church about a Divorce Care Course and am trying not to keep everything bottled up inside of me.

It hurts and I feel completely numb inside, is it shock, is it sadness or is it just feeling sorry for myself, I don't know. I am simply trying to take one day, and sometimes when it really gets bad, one hour at a time. I miss physical contact and I miss the hugs from friends and at the same time I want to avoid it for fear of being hurt again.

I am not attending my old church, I somehow doubt I will be able to return there for a very long time if ever. I have 3 homes in Johannesburg that I go to so that I am not alone, I hate silence and I cannot be alone, it hurts more.

Am I angry with God? I do not know, I haven't got there yet.

This week I must contact the lawyer to begin the divorce proceedings.

Thank you

Down Syndrome

Hey guys, I am not breathing at the moment. All I do now is survive and go through the motions and try and create a routine that will get me to tomorrow. There is no next week yet, no next month, and no next year.

Today is too steep but I move forward. I must survive and recover and become more than I was so that I can be all that is required of the angels that wait for me.

I want to love again, to feel to touch to laugh. If this is possible or meant to be, I am not sure. Will I ever be able to commit again? I don't know. Does that mean I do not try? No. I seek no answers, I simply carry on till I break down and then I get up and move again. I cannot feel God but I hope He is around the corner waiting smiling with arms open. I do not enjoy the day and despise the evenings.

I am unable to pray or question or reason. It is not that I do not want to, I simply cannot. I eat when I remember because I was told that I must and even them there is no taste or pleasure. Perhaps death would have been easier because I would not feel I could have done more, loved more, given more. Please do not share my feelings beyond yourselves, I have sent this message to the Megaw's because they enquired of me. This is not me vs Heather, this is me getting over this and getting better for me and my angels. I cannot type anymore. I am crying and tired and must rest. I will call you both but not this week.

Hello Darkness my new Fiend

It is absolutely amazing, my chest tightens, I breathe shallower and this is how another night approaches.

The writing helps but only the next day; tonight it helps kill time. Last night was the worst, it seemed to pull me deeper and deeper and somehow I knew that the bottom was not in sight yet.

How did I know this, because I still fight it. I fight back the tears and try and stifle the sobs. Maybe I am embarrassed, maybe I still do not believe it, maybe I am only starting this walk and am dreading it.

You are all amazing and I am still confounded that anyone would want to journey with me on this trip of despair and heartache. God has sent you to catch me with prayers when I can no longer hold on; is this because I cannot face Him yet? Is it because I am not ready for the next step, oh please God do not tell me it gets worse! What is left to be broken? Night destroys me and day attempts to build me up for the next bombardment. Where is my fortress where I am to hide and rest and recover? What goes through my head when I am driving home in the dark is "As I walk through the Valley of the Shadow of Death..." and the rest seems to vanish.

Where is my comfort?
Where is my armour?
Where is my shield?

I feel bruised and tired and can hear the laughter as I try and stand up, and I must stand up or am I meant to stay down?

I was comforted today and had to fight back tears twice. Am I meant to weep openly in public? Is that what is required before I can continue to the next phase of my new hell? Is there a sequence I am meant to follow? Are there rules for this or are they made up as I go along?

When I close my eyes I see my angels and I have to open them again, I miss them more than life itself. How can I comfort them and hold them when I cannot even contemplate how I will face this night, darker than the last.

I do not want to reach out in case I cannot let go, I do not want to smother and scare those who see me and do not recognise me. I need to know that it will cease and somehow believe it, why does that seem so hard?

Saturday I must collect my clothes, my few personal belongings and my wedding ring. I have not worn it since June but the imprint of 20 years is still on my hand, I see it EVERY SINGLE DAMN DAY when I am driving, it has not faded, it is as clear as if I have only now removed it.

Enough for tonight, the battles begins and I must face my new enemy, he has already won tonight but I will fight anyway. I have no choice it is the only way I know how.

Goodnight till tomorrow...

Demons from my past

I *was convinced that this particular beast had been buried and forgotten, yet tonight it not only showed its teeth it attacked as well. I was not prepared and thus not armed and worst of all no armour on. As if I had not enough on my plate it had to appear TONIGHT. My heart raced my mouth dried and my brain went ballistic. I was scared and instantly convinced that this was now truly the end. You all jumped in, why would you do that? I had basically resigned from the game, this one broke my back and I could not get up again. You and my God appeared again. Why won't you stay? I so need you now. Please hang around this time, I need to see you hear you feel you. Tell me it will all be ok, tell me there is an end in sight. Tell me I will love again one day when I am no longer broken and bruised. Is this possible? The silence again. Sigh sleep where o where is your mercy? Take me now I beg you, keep me safe till daylight caresses me once again.*

Till morning cruel world...

A Life Without Love is Not a Life

Ever seen that lonely person wandering aimlessly round the shopping centre, the lady drinking a cup of tea alone just staring off into the distance, the guy in the bookshop checking out books? Ever stopped to take a second glance or just passed them by as you deal with them? Ever wondered what they are thinking about?

What about the father with the kids carrying the bags and scurrying from shop to shop? Ever thought twice about the person in the car that wont smile back at you and just seems to see right through you?

I am all of the above; I live that nightmare. I wonder from book to book not even focusing on the titles, I don't drink coffee unless it is at home because I am not comfortable with my own company. I do not enjoy spending time with me; I would not want to be friends with me at the moment.

I spent an hour in the shopping centre today and left depressed and lonely. I could not wait to get back to the cocoon of safety of my car, hiding behind my sunglasses and loud emo rock that drowns out any thoughts or contact that might get through. Is it because I want to avoid contact or is it simply that I am afraid that my waves of emotions might somehow drown that sweet old lad next to me, or awaken a sleeping child from a sleep so peaceful it seems angelic. Or drain the life and joy from friends like a starving vampire devouring an innocent soul.

My eyes are old, aged with tears, aged with sorrow, weary almost feeling like they have expired and need to thrown out and replaced. My mouth is continually dry, I try to lick my lips but there is no saliva in my mouth, I try and drink but it does not quench my thirst, I remain thirsty.

Loneliness is like being stranded in the middle of a desert in the midst of a raging sandstorm, even though there might be someone an arms length away, you are not aware of them

Does it end here? Fortunately not.

After initially being told that the they could not spend tonight with me, Nicole who was unaware of the situation asked Mom if she could go to Dad tonight. I saw an incoming call from Heather and after being shouted at and threatened (she did sms and apologise an hour later) I reluctantly answered. Imagine my surprise when I heard Nicole on the line asking if I could come fetch her.

She is now sitting next to me playing on her cellphone.

Simonne is apparently angry with me, but that is tomorrow's challenge.

Midnight Heroin

I tried not to meet you tonight, I tried to sleep without your aid, I thought that if my young angel was next to me I could rest, but alas the sadness and despair are all inside. They spread like smoke filling a room filling every corner smothering and suffocating. You gasp and your chest tightens. So I reluctantly turn to you, my sleep heroin, my killer of all dreams of all emotion, my midnight friend. Do thy deed, I have no further need for this world tonight. I was shouted at and threatened today, she apologised but the scar and memory remain, is this a glimpse of the road ahead? Why have you not suffocated me, enough take me now, tomorrow we rise again. But tonight I surrender...

Midnight Heroin II

So here we go again, not even the midnight heroin brings its sweet comfort tonight, my stomach is empty I should have eaten but was barely able to swallow half a slice of bread. 3 hours of tears and no relief, but sweet knowledge that He does care, The desire to see him face to face is not granted and in a way I am pleased, I would not be able to look him in the eye not tonight. My chest is tight, my breathing is shallow my jaw is tight my eyes are burning. I long for arms to hold me to comfort me and a voice to tell me that it will all be alright. The sheer desolation and loneliness is dragging me down again to the depths of hell and I cannot fight it. I need a hand to grasp to hang onto to stop me falling further, a warm hand. Even though I walk through the Valley of the Shadow of Death, I am trying to keep believing that You have not abandoned me. You have to be my shepherd. Today the harsh reality begins with the first visit to the lawyer. I am petrified and wish I could turn and run and just keep running and running and running. I am not happy with this hand life has dealt me, I want to feel anything absolutely anything. I do not want to be lonely anymore. I want to switch this night off and recharge for just now, but the night it seems enjoys my torment. So I reluctantly fight back the tears and the oncoming headache and pray for some kind of comfort. Your prayers and thoughts will never be forgotten and I could never ever repay you. Thank you and bless you, I have nothing to offer but tears and sadness. I can offer no joy or happiness or any constructive promise of hope. It is so very very dark and so very very cold and lonely. Let me leave and retire to my own misery.

Good morning Monday, goodbye Sunday.

Single

Where to start, lots of laughter, joking and smiling. Cooking a meatball pasta meal and watching a family eat it. No I did not have any. Having supper with old friends who have become new again and sharing and caring and not crying. Seeing families that work despite the pressures of life and little girls with a twinkle in their eyes. Holding hands and saying grace in homes where God is still alive and part of life. Chatting to my angels on Mxit while I drained pasta and added the finished sauce. Laughing with each other over a sms, would be much better to have them closer. Realising that Divorce is not a sin but that which leads up to it is. I headed off for a run when I felt the depression began to attack and did some weights afterwards, my muscles ache but it is nice. For red wine and a lovely meal and honesty between friends, for a friend that stopped working to help a confused friend with am email and another who was a sms away from a saddened heart at 22h30 in the night. These are what makes this bearable, I found myself shouting and swearing at people on the road today, they were most probably no worse than any other day. Memories haunt me when perhaps they should perhaps encourage me, but at least there are memories. I have not embraced anger yet, but the cracks are emerging and I cannot keep it under chain much longer. Please be close when it bursts through. I am lonely. I do not wish to stop talking or for folk to leave, if only they could stay and chat till I have fallen asleep. All about me isn't it! Is this wrong? Am I meant to stop feeling sorry for myself? Is this normal? What is normal anymore? Too much for tonight. A doctors visit for next week. Info for Simon about Contact lenses. A debt counselor that answers their phone would be nice. And a promise made to a 11 year old that this weekend would be filled with fun fun fun. Goodnight my friends. I wonder if Heather is alone and sleeping.

Alone Tonight

I am alone. Yes I know that is a simple statement that requires no explanation, but let me explain if I may. I want a hand to hold. This is not a sexual desire, this is not a cry from my loins but from my heart. I miss holding hands, it sounds so blatantly irrelevant and unimportant yet it makes me so desperately sad that I have lost this privilage. I want to hold someones hand and just close my eyes and enjoy it. I not only want to, but so wish to have this dream fulfilled that it has driven me to tears. What a simple gesture that we take so for granted? Please can I have it back? It might even stop the tears. Please.

Sanity Perhaps

A long long day that involved hitting a real low point at about 11h00 and meant driving with tears in my eyes, sounds like a song doesn't it? It was not a good day but somehow ended on a positive note.

We had a discussion that didn't start well and then I proceeded to tell Heath exactly how I felt, that I was on medication for depression and had to take sleeping tablets to try and get to sleep every, a schedule 5 tablet. I only took a schedule 5 because I was not aware that there was in fact a schedule 7. :-)

I then proceeded to tell her about crying and needing to be near friends permanently, of how I felt when I walked into what used to be our home which we had built and accumulated over 23 years of togetherness and saw her and Deon living the happy family in what used to be our home.

I told her that I would not be setting foot on the property again and definitely not in the house at all. I have given my keys to Simon and did not want them back.

I told Heath that I was not at all happy that Deon was sleeping over and found it unacceptable and how would she have felt if the situation was reversed and she discovered that I was sleeping with my girlfriend with my daughters in the room next door. Her response saddened me greatly.

To cut a long story short, I received a sms from Deon saying that he would not be sleeping over till things were finalised and hoped we could still be friends one day!!!!!!!!!!!!!!!!!!!!!

Heath phoned me a few minutes later in tears and asked if I minded if he came to visit her at home, I explained to her that I could not control her personal life just as she could not control mine. I told her that I had no problem with Deon coming over to visit, but I had a huge problem with him sleeping over.

PS. Thanks Candy, he is no longer a friend on FB

Good night my friends and God willing tonight we sleep. If not expect sms's any time from 23h00

Reflections

Well another day down and one more sleep till I get to see my babies and hold them again.

This was the week that was and has and shall remain to be.

Lots of anger this week, lots of deep consideration and what if's.

Reflections of what used to be, reflections of the life I used to see, what if and whatever. Phone calls to folk and from folk in times of darkness and always being so very amazed of the workings of the Christian circle and body.

It still hurts but there seems to be a peace about certain aspects and I might be able to start a conversation with God this weekend. It's not that I have forgotten how to pray but it all just seems to be different, almost like a different plane, not sure if this makes sense. Fortunately it is my theory and it makes sense for me.

I was asked by someone today if I could forgive the parties concerned and my answer made me think for a while. Yes to one and not quite the other yet. Forgive yes but unfortunately not forget.

The emotions are still very raw and still so very very much to process that I can now understand that it would take a fair amount of time to deal with it.

Anger has certainly reared its head and this has been alarming in the rate it has accelerated. I am finding that the exercise certainly assists in channeling it. This year, baby steps, 2011, Comrades ha ha

So where to from here? Well it's Simon, Nicole and Ted, with a little help from an awesome group of friends against the world. Why will we succeed? Not because of our awesomeness, but because of His Love.

Let me attempt this ritual we casually refer to as sleep, for I fear that it has lost its stranglehold on my life and is now merely a distant relative popping in for a cup of tea.

Good night God Bless and chat soon, like maybe now if Teddy goes emo on all of us again!

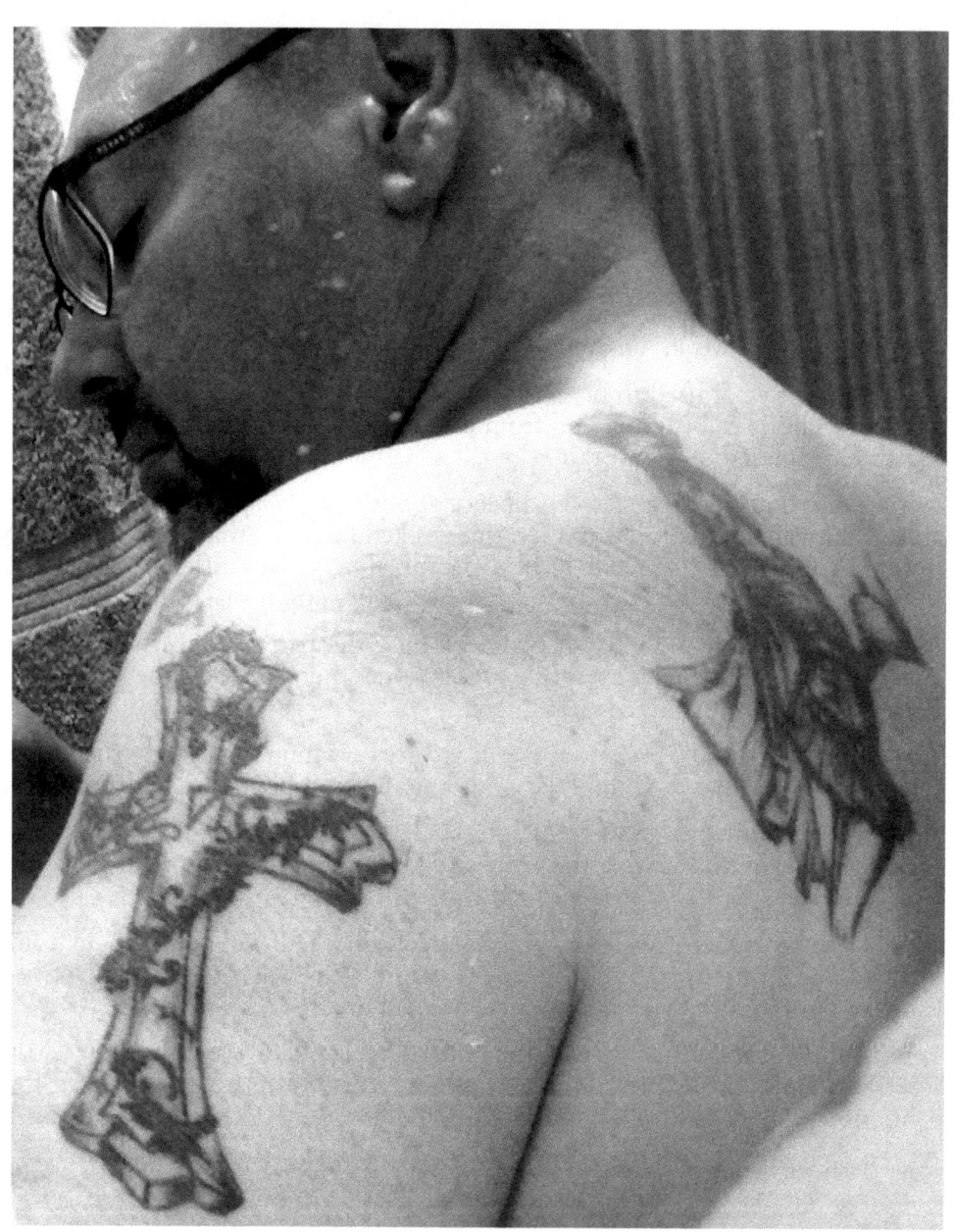

Tonight

Where to begin? I discovered that I was able to forgive one member of the party, that I was able to begin to pray again even if they were only short prayers and not really conversations yet. I am not able to forgive Deon yet for the manner in which the whole incident occurred, it just seemed to be so masterfully planned. Or am I just imagining it? I lost my car radio today, it was not so much the loss as the violation once more of my privacy. There is no safe haven at the moment, nothing that seems untouchable, definitely no place to hide and nowhere to run. I cannot escape this and must therefore continue to plod along and face my emotions. Yes I am still overcome with guilt for the time I am stealing from those around me that offer so much and ask for nothing in return. Thinking that by having my girls would somehow make it easier, the joy of having them around is amazing but when the lights go out its pretty much the same. How much longer, no idea I suppose; the answer would be as long as it takes. I yearn for company, I yearn for the presence of folk next to me, not even to talk just to be close. When I cry the touch of a hand on the shoulder is the most reassuring feeling around, seems sad to be so lonely when you have so many who care. I am still exhausted and not eating properly and need to address this, surely a responsible adult would be able to resolve this easily? It is late and the house is still, still around me. Sleep and I sit huddled over my cellphone, too scared to lie down. How much longer? Does it get better and if so when? I realised today that nothing will ever seem normal again, it has all changed and God willing for the better, time my friend will tell. I must lie down, I must sleep, I am utterly exhausted and my tablet is taking effect.

Good night my friends, sweet dreams...

Crying

Why have I entitled tonight 'crying'? Well, it has become such a relevant part of my life that I seem to find tears all around me.

Tonight I had Nicole crying on the phone for me and begging me to come collect her. I see the tears in friends eyes and it is almost as if I am passing on my misery to them. In fact they are simply sharing my sorrow willingly. This is not understandable for me and as such I am unable to reason with it, unable to put it in a box and file it away.

I went for a medical today to replace existing drugs with new chemicals that will hopefully make me an easier person to live with for those who are in contact with me and most importantly for me. I am not a great fan of who I am, I realise that I am a new work in the making, but do not like who I am presently. A friend informed me politely this evening that I am a bit of a control freak. Never thought that that was a bad thing! lol

I am hoping that God is breaking me down to make more of the person He wants me to be and less of the person I want to be. Am I ready for this? NO! I still fight this daily and am very aware that this is something I have to deal with. There is no quick fix, this is years of me being unravelled and I have no control over it, God has decided that it is now the time for Him to do after years of me trying to do it my way.

I am tired, emotionally drained, confused and unbalanced.

I have begun running again with a friend who has stepped up to the plate and asked questions no-one else has. They are not easy to answer and in fact for many of them I have no answer.

I have another friend who challenges me with questions and statements about what God is doing in my life, another who challenges my attitude and progression and just listens when I have to get the madness out of head and just put words in the silence. I HATE SILENCE!

I saw a GP today who asked me How I was really feeling? My answer, I could burst into tears right now, I am Broken.

I receive sms's about websites that offer easy quick divorces, 23 yrs to instant removal. This hurts in a different way. Why would one that loved and cared now want to remove and erase so frantically?

My blood pressure is slightly high but acceptable, I have to eat in the morning to take my medication. I have to sleep to cope with my depression which it seems is the underlying root of all the problems. A bigger medical is scheduled for 28 days time.

A debt counsellor has been contacted and a meeting is scheduled.

A call needs to made tomorrow for me to see a professional who will God willing assist me with anger and some other issues that have taken me to new depths of despair. Anger!

What happened to innocence?

What happened to morality?

What happened to for better or worse?

What happened oh please tell me what happened?

We are living in a decaying society where if we do not have the light and guidence and hope that is promised to us, we have nothing.

Each morning I arise hoping for some ray of hope only to end it at the moment tired and sad. Yes there are moments of joys, but they seem to be smothered by the other stuff. It would be wonderful to see the tide turn.

I prayed for a sobbing angel tonight, I prayed for a lost soul and I might have prayed for myself, but I cannot remember.

It is over, I now wish for sleep, deep restful sleep, in fact any sleep will do!

Tonight

It never dawned on me that it has all been happening for far too long.

Do we become so acclimatised to our surroundings that we become unaware of the chaos around us. Are we so insensitive to the madness and pain that we just build a wall around us that shields us and we continue with happy faces and false laughs irrespective of the fact that we are slowing killing that which brought us joy in the beginning.

I am by now insinuating that I am the victim in this situation; it is the perhaps a combination of life, stress and circumstances that led to a breakdown in communication and ultimately disaster.

Could I have intervened? Of course. Could I have foreseen the inevitable? Well perhaps, but there were other circumstances.

Do I accept blame and guilt, somewhat, but definitely not all.

Tomorrow I have my very first encounter with a psychologist and this has to be a step in the right direction, God willing. Until 6 months ago I would not have been seen dead in a Mind Magician's offices, but how the tables have turned.

How much have I pushed and ignored and denied that it caused a relationship to deteriorate to such a level that shouting was required?

I could just walk away from it in the past, but now it is too much. I can simply switch off and enjoy the silence, but the silence disappears at 02h00 in the morning and the scene replays itself again and again and again.

This has perhaps being ongoing for 4 years, 4 YEARS and I did not see the writing on the wall. Why oh why did I not address it sooner?

The damage is far from done, there are still many consequences and heartaches and tears to be shed. Many what if's and if only's. A minute sometimes seems like an hour.

Prayer. What is it? Is it talking or listening or both? There is no silence, so to listen is extremely difficult, almost impossible; in fact not possible at all. The pictures spin through my head like a one arm bandit and when they stop they make no sense at all. Sometimes they slow down and I can make some sense of it all, but then it all descends into fast forward mode. I am in fact a hamster on a wheel and as fast as I run to reach my goal as fast it runs ahead of me. I give up, collapse and fall into restless sleep only to awaken and repeat the whole cycle again in the morning.

So I pray when prompted, I pray when my angels cry, I pray when I get angry but it is not a 2 way conversation, it is a shout, a sob, a plea and sometimes a wish.

There is no peace yet, only anger, pain, confusion and relief when another days ceases to be. There is no joy, comfort, rest or passion only survival.

I long to laugh honestly. I was asked by my new Dr when we were chatting and joking how do I really feel? I have become so trained in concealing my emotions that I can cover or disguise them that most folk would not be aware of what turmoil lies beneath. I answered that I was broken but intent on getting better. I explained that my angels required me to function and that was why I had no problem getting up in the morning.

I have the choice not to be shouted at anymore. Likewise you have the choice not to put up with your situation. You can say "NO" and address the issue. My choice is no longer relationship threatening. Please oh please do not let it get to that stage.

Goodnight my extremely blessed friends, God Bless and thank you for hearing my ramblings.

Ted

P.S. I will not be shouted at!

Mind Mechanics vs. Storm Running

Ok so I got the time wrong for the meeting with the therapist, arrived an hour early and had to go away and come back again. Not the best start to an appointment I was not looking forward to

To put you in the picture, I would rather be tackled by Bakkies Botha and Schalk Burger that go to the dentist or see a therapist.

Who knows what they might find? Maybe I was deprived of ice cream at the age of 3 and there is no way back. So it wasn't what I expected, some prompting, some questions and an hour later it was over. No tears, no mind bending headaches, no vomiting. Well, this is my first time and I did not know what to accept.

So what came out of the session;

I am a bit of a control freak (no laughing please)

I have difficulty showing my emotions

I keep things bottled up

I tend to want to help other people and have difficulty accepting help

I am dealing with anger issues and seemingly have difficulty expressing or releasing it.

My anger is directed at individuals and might very well be directed at God, but this box has not been opened yet

Ah boxes, I classify everything in boxes and prefer to only have a certain number of boxes open at a time (yes so that I can control it)

Lists—I have rules, some negotiable some not (I will come back to these)

My faith is very important to me

My girls are very important to me

My friends are very important to me

My values and integrity are very important to me

Rules: (in no particular order)

1. Your friend's partner is off limits—ALWAYS
2. Loyalty, Faithfulness and Trust in a relationship are non-negotiable
3. Friends don't steal from friends
4. Love is sacred
5. Church is questionable but God is forever
6. Luke Watson is a poephol
7. You hurt my girls I will hurt you worse
8. If I have something and you need it, it's yours
9. ...more to follow

Anger Management

Running is good, boxing bag is good, writing is good. Writing a list of what makes me angry when I think about a specific person is good and is a list that I should also begin.

So I went for a run in a storm, well I only got the end bit of the storm. The idea of jogging in a storm seems to appeal to me :-) not sure why but I have this vision of running in storms all over the place, there must be some deep hidden meaning, bet the therapists are loving this. lol

It was a good run, sore, tiring and my back is sore—yes I suppose I run funny and maybe the gasping for air and bulging eyes might scare small animals and children, but hey they should not be out in the storm anyway.

My girls were treated to a haircut by a good friend today, Bless you and they were so happy like princesses and kept following routes that included mirrors so they could check it out. Got home and my dog came running for love and promptly got into the car with me. Miss my dog a LOT.

So how was my day? I did not really have time to think much today, it all seemed very busy, How do I feel? Tired.

Oh yes, apparently the fact that I stayed in the house for 4 months with Heather and Deon coming over to visit was not beneficial to a healthy state of being - go figure!

Well, I sort of expect a bit of a melt-down this weekend, it will be the first one in a month without my angels so I am going to try and stay as busy as possible, but I can feel the pressure building and the dam walls are a gonna blow baby.

In conclusion, thank you thank you thank you for all of you who have been part of my journey, your caring, prayers, conversations, encouragement, hugs and company have pulled me through month 1.

Lists

So I started my lists today. 3 lists and lots me things that need doing. Why did I start them, well... Have been feeling really joyous the last 2 days and could feel myself slipping into a horrible place again. I know that this is part of the process but I do not want to be there now, please not now. So when things got dark and claustrophobic I had to find something to somehow drag me to some sort of sanity. Lists. Yup lists. I did one for the lawyers meeting on Monday morning, I am definitely not looking forward to that. My fear is that it will lead to unnecessary conflict and I am so tired of conflict. 2 was a list to discuss with the debt counsellor. Just could not get together this week so next week it will have be and finally list no 3 a list of things to do in the future, my fun list. This includes things that I want to do with my girls, specific things to do with specific friends and things I want to do. Things that people roll their eyes at, things that people click their tongues at and things that will just make me happy, like running in storms :) o sleep where is your sweet kiss, I yearn for you but you evade me. I must leave you and begin this wrestling match now for it is late and tomorrow beckons.

Goodnight my friends...

Emotional Bouncing

*I*f the piano in the Track 'New Moon' by Alexandre Despat is a weapon of despair then each note is a small pin driving into my heart. Each note brings a drying in the back of my throat and my eyes grow weary and slightly moist. The lack of words makes it seem more fragile, hollow, more direct as it slowly unwraps the steel cage I have placed around my heart. The slow removal rips away from the wall of the heart and as I bleed, I can almost feel emotions easing out. They are not joy love peace compassion, instead they are grief sorrow loneliness, the sorts of emotions a damaged hurt animal would experience in the wild. I have been hunted, wounded and now I hide as I await healing to take place. For survival to take place, I must recover. It would be easier to just give in but the survival instinct is too strong. But is it really? Or is it merely that I am guided somehow led to the next round of bruising life encounters of the reality kind? I long so desperately for someone to hold whilst I sob and sleep my way through the months ahead, but that would be a blessing too great to imagine. So I continue moving, whether it is forward or backwards I am not sure, but I reassure myself that motion will keep me active and keep those dark brooding demons away. I have no strength for them now. I feel no anger today, only sadness regret and a great sense of loss. I miss what I can no longer have, I miss what I used to take for granted. I miss my life, my family, my home, my dog. I miss the chaos of a seemingly strange family enviroment, I miss life, what I have now is not God-like, this is hell and I . . . must suck it up and move on. The Lodewijks Men do not feel sorry for themselves, they hide their emotions and get stuff done. But my stuff has been taken from me, what does a Lodewijks man do now? Too many thoughts, too few answers, too many emotions and no end of the tunnel in sight. Silence introduces new partners none of them friendly, it is time to get out of this tomb and drive anywhere, just drive...

Summons

So Ted, what did you do today?

Well now that you ask, I decided to beat myself up again emotionally. lol

I worked until 12 because hey still need some money even though I am not Rockefeller, yup just the other fella.

I went to the lawyer today to collect my summons and sign it only to find that I had to in fact take the summons issued to me by Heather to the Sheriff of the Court in the middle of Johannesburg and give it to them. So an hour and 20 minutes later after 2 police road blocks and a very hot little Fiat Uno whose engine fan was working overtime, I arrived at the sheriff of the court. No horses outside, no Clint Eastwood lookalikes not even a sheriff impersonator, nope nothing.

A friendly lady directed me upstairs to a little lady bordering on midget size who took the summons, typed something and then issued me with MY OWN SUMMONS!!!!!

I SUMMONED MYSELF !!!! ARGGHHHHHH

Then I took all of this back to what used to be my lawyer (now Heather's lawyer) and dropped it all off. I served myself.

How sad is that. It also took up 2 and a half hours of my day. Sigh.

Now the divorce machine shifts into top gear and all going according to plan, on the 11th of December 2009, I will be divorced. That apparently is the same as single, a bachelor.

It cannot be referred to as unmarried or can it? I mean I was married, but now am not or will not be on the 11th, for now I am separated.

It is all a bit much and I am confused about a lot.

For instance, if you love someone with all your heart and then you separate, do they keep some of your heart?

Does that mean that your heart has less capacity to love in the future?

What happens to that portion you have lost?

Are you able to love the same? I somehow want to believe that you can love again, but presently I am not able to comprehend that. I spoke to a friend who had 3 husbands, after each divorce she jumped straight into another relationship. Now she is single and she says that she is content?

I want more than content.

I want to love again.

I want a second chance.

But what if this was the one and only and I blew it? Well then I suppose I will have to be content and focus on my girls. It does not make sense and the more I contemplate, the more complex the scenario.

Clarity and peace, what a glorious combination, what a blessing that would be. To be rid of the spinning and buzzing in my head, the knot in my stomach and the lump in my throat, that would be nice. Nice would be fantastic at the moment.

Last night I had supper with an old friend, it was good.

Tonight I meet with a young couple who are newer friends, it will be interesting, I have a policy now that no question is too personal or private and I wonder who will ask what and when. My only condition is that the really personal questions be asked face to face, I want to look into the eyes of the person asking to be sure that they are sincere.

Tomorrow I am hoping to have supper with a friend, old and very special who has suffered and lost more than I could ever contemplate, I expect it to be a very emotional and hard evening for me.

Did he get angry with God?

Did he doubt all he came to accept as cast in stone?

Did he ever question his sanity?

How did he survive?

Did he ever consider running away? (Where would he run to?)

Does he have a safe place he can go to, is there place for me there to?

How much suffering is enough?

Questions but no answers and I have so many, millions it seems. I am angry at the church yet they have not done me wrong?

I am saddened by my lack of faith and my inability to move through this process quicker, yet I believe God is trying to remould me. So should I be saddened or just patient?

Does any of this make any sense to anyone because to me it just gives me headache and makes me tired?

Forgive me. I cannot anymore today.

The Week that was!

It began on Sunday with the panic setting in for the lawyers meeting on Monday. Why was I nervous? Well, my fear that it would result in a fight, an argument and I do not really have the strength to fight at this stage. It doesn't mean that I am weak just tired. I could still fight, that I have no doubt about. Well, this is not making any sense.

I am also sad. It is the end of an era, 23 years 19 married and 4 dating and tether is no more.

I still battle to comprehend the world without Heather at my side. I know that the reality of the divorce is so near and that there is no chance of reconciliation, but it still is so hard to unwind the bond that has held us together through so much for so long. I suppose the thought that after what we had lived through and experienced, the love we had received from others and in turn given, the fact that we understood each other so well that often we acted without thinking and as a team could do almost everything... well almost everything except keep the marriage going.

I understand that it takes 2 to cause it to fall apart, I understand that there could have been reconciliation, I understand that I am not entirely to blame, I even understand that God loves and forgives me for my part in it, yet I am battling with guilt like you cannot believe.

If only I had shared my feelings
If only I had been a better listener
If only I had been more supportive
If only I had not made the financial decisions that put me in the predicament I find myself in now
If only if only

Let me jump to my meeting with Regan on Thursday, or as she herewith be known as "My Cynical Psychopath". What a chat it was, the essence of the chat was that I was not responsible for all of this, I had responsibilities and no, I did not have to be a Mom and a Dad. The girls had a Mom that needed to fulfill that role, I had to be their Dad and the best damn Dad I could be and that is what I am working towards. I would concentrate on that and make sure that my times with the girls were memorable and meaningful, this does not detract from the fact that my responsibilities fell away, I was still responsible for discipline, spiritual guidance and fatherly advice. I need to continue to build the type of relationship that allows them to respect my opinions, but also allows them to share any news with me be it good or not so good. I am fortunate that there is in fact a solid foundation in place and I need to keep building on it.

Other issues addressed were "Health" which at this stage is pretty much under control, I am doing and seeing and medicating and exercising so it is a planned action routine that is working well at the moment. Eating is slightly better, I have developed a passion for salad, go figure and will continue to work towards balance eating ha ha.

Depression

Wow, that really hit BEEEG time, man oh man and what a low we had this week. It was awful, just horrible and low and black. Can't really think of what to compare it with, it was like sinking in quicksand and just sinking lower and lower. There was no bottom, just when it seemed like this was it, it would drag you lower, my chest tightens and

Back to Monday and the first visit to the lawyer who is now Heather's lawyer and Heather who is suing me for divorce. I am battling with the emotional politically correctiveness that would define the correct behavior in this context. Let me try and explain in plain English; because Heather is now suing me, she is responsible for the most of the divorce process. She had to fill in the documentation and this must have been difficult for her as she was crying whilst doing it. No I didn't laugh at her, Wayne, lol, I went to get some tissues and because I thought a hug would not be appropriate (what the hell is appropriate in this mixed up life of mine?), I sort of rubbed her on the shoulder quickly and thought, "That was encouraging."

We managed to chat civilly and that I think somehow makes it harder. Perhaps a fight might have been easier. There is no right way to do this, it all just feels awkward and polite and I am wanting to keep the conversations as short as possible, perhaps the shorter they are the less chance I will have to say how I really feel. I somehow still want to protect and shield Heather from as much as possible, it is almost a built in coping mechanism. I battle not to see her as a unit with my girls, my 3 girls. I realize that this is no longer possible and that that dream has been shattered and lies about me like a chandelier that has crashed onto a black marble floor, I am somehow still trying to pick up some of the pieces and put them into some sort of order that I can control. All I succeed in doing is to cut myself on the broken pieces and now I bleed and gaze confused at the scene around me. There are still moments of shock and disbelief followed by moments of focused determination as I attempt to focus on the future and somehow attempt to juggle the chaos. One day at a time and when it gets a little rough around the edges, then thanks, Candy, one hour at a time.

Monday after the lawyers was followed by a panic attack at the Leff House, I was shaking like a leaf and still managed to fight back the tears, I just cannot let go completely what the hell is wrong with me? I finished Monday evening with supper with an old friend and that was encouraging.

Tuesday was a disaster! I was under the impression that I would simply be collecting my summons from the lawyer, taking it to the police station and getting it signed. Nope, it had to go to the sheriff of the court in the middle of Johannesburg, be given to him so that he in turn could issue it back to me and then I would take this all back to the lawyer. Two and a half hours of frustration, sadness and on top of it loss of earnings which I can ill afford. Lovely day.

Supper with Craig and Gen and then sleep.

Thursday was my counseling session and this was one of the few highlights of the week, some clarity at last, some coping mechanisms, some news that certainly enabled me to face Thursday. This might help with slowing down the mad reeling pictures in my head, by focusing on what can be dealt with and putting aside the issues that are untouchable at the moment.

Friday and Heather has a new puppy, a stray her boss found, she has decided to keep it, in my opinion not the wisest decision with 2 dogs already at home, a new job and uncertainty about the house/accommodation. But yes I hear all of you, not my problem!

Girls with me for the weekend so that is encouraging and enjoyable and awesome.

So what is the prospect for the week ahead.

We have the 1 hour meeting where we sit and finalize the divorce agreement and put in all the details, this I assume is the official document that will be with us for the rest of our lives or until the girls are of such an age that they no longer require support. Not sure when that would be?

The one point that was in the summons was the sole custody and the fact that Heather has full decision on the girls religious decisions, this I am unable to accept. I have certain responsibilities as a father that I am not prepared to sign away in a legal document. I trust that this will not be an issue and if it is, then I can see it delaying the divorce and that is too bad.

On the work front, my CV has been sent out and I am hoping to hear this week, God willing this will come through. It will guarantee me at least 4 and a half days work a week. This will provide a more solid base to launch my new life from and allow me sort of freedom to rebuild and restructure.

The Week Ahead

1. Lawyer Meeting on Monday
   The deciding document and the race down to the divorce finishing line – madness sadness and the end of a 2 decades.

2. Job Prospect
   Please please please

3. I don't know

I am sorry but that is as far as I can go, just pray for the above 2 and then I can move on to more. Perhaps just a reprieve from the depression, especially after dropping my girls at school tomorrow, then straight to the lawyers and then straight to the Heineken site for 6 hours of inspections and paperwork. Long day.

Thank you so much for your continued prayers and blessings, they are not ever taken for granted and will not be forgotten.

Today

Today, I signed my Divorce Agreement

Today, I ignored a woman I used to love deeply

Today I received back the right to decide on my girls lives including their religious rights

Today I moved back out on my own again

Today... today I embraced loneliness by choice again

23 November 2009, the day Heather and I signed our divorce papers and the lawyers started processing the divorce in earnest.

Today, the day Heather said that she was getting "screwed" in the divorce, I offered to swop all my debt for her house. I was not taken up on the offer.

Today is the first day of the rest of my life—a cliché perhaps a very very real reality.

I sit alone and realize that I have friends, friends who care and pray for me, friends that communicate with me.

I have girls who need their Dad to be healthy and strong. I explained to Simon that I was having a bad day yesterday and she hugged me and told me it was ok and she loves me. I am blessed. I went for a walk with Nicole and we looked at 2 houses I could not afford, but we had fun. We dreamt a little and forgot about life and divorce for a while.

A friend who could not afford to offer me money did, I declined but felt blessed.

I feel as if I could make this life thing work again and instantly realize that I am scared to be overly optimistic, reality is only an emotion away.

I am secretly okay for now and I praise God for my now.

Goodnight...

Love

How simple is first love, smiles, giggles, the excitement and electricity of that touch. Holding your breath during that first kiss praying you do not mess it up, praying your breath doesn't smell.

Holding hands and smiling a lot, staring into each others' eyes and hugs that you never wanted to end. Feeling as if your heart would break if you didn't see each other each day. To touch the face of the one you love and be happy, be content, be excited.

Listening to music and the words meaning something to you, giving or receiving flowers, talking and laughing and smiling a lot.

Falling asleep in one another's arms, the scent of a loved one that special smell that lingers in their hair, on their clothes on their lips. Just lying together and looking at the sky looking at stars and dreaming of the future dreaming of planning a future.

Eating a meal however simple or sophisticated at a candle lit table and making small talk. Smiles that reach all the way from your eyes to your heart and tingle. Walks that you never want to end, slow dances that require no music. Innocent hugs and passionate embraces.

What makes this all possible is someone to share it with, joy love sorrow passion.

All better with someone special.

Dating

So the weekend is basically done and dusted and I worked most of it.

Only ate a energy bar today and then had a friend with a beer and hungry was I . . . well something like that so rushed over to the Leffs for a quick burger and then went home to the flat. Prior to that I had 2 beers with an old friend, realized we have known each other for about 20 odd years, he offered to help me service the Uno at his cost, an amazing blessing out of the blue, we really do serve an awesome God who never fails to amaze me.

And then I received a ladies cellphone number and was asked to give her a call if I was not taken, taken, what is taken? I feel like a piece of meat. lol

It was a shock and a surprise at the same time and then suddenly the prospect of a possible date was alarming and very scary at the same time.

I thought my shelf life was past due and did not even consider the possibility of dating for a very very long time. Time will tell I suppose

Dating continued . . .

How do you do and oh hello so please to meet you I have to go
Would love to stay and have a drink but can feel my cheeks turning pink
Not that I'm scared but it's all very new
It's really me and so not you
I am not sure of the dating game and am so sorry what is your name
I did not know please do not cry yes of course the cow had to die
It's called a steak and I know you care
Please stop screaming it's a little rare
Oh dear I fear this may not go well
I have created a dating nightmarish hell
But when the time is right I pray
I'll know what to do and what to say

So time to call it a night even though it is only 19H00, a new week beckons and I must have something to eat before Deanne finds out and I get lectured lol...

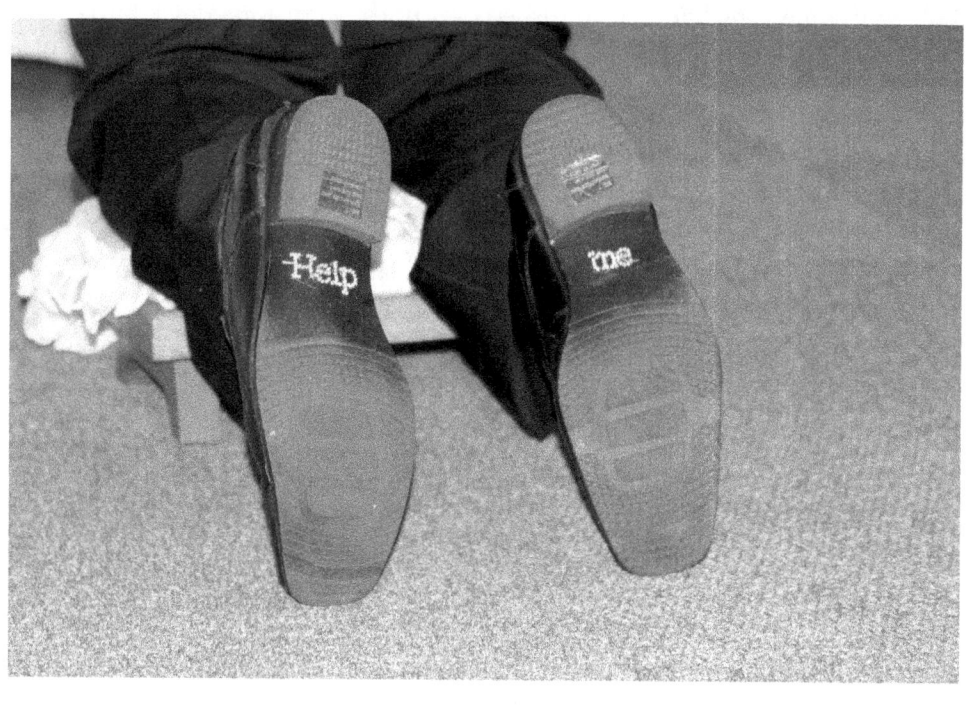

Wednesday is Near

Options Response

I realized yesterday afternoon that I have not yet dealt with the anger and that I have been kidding myself that it is only directed to him, there is anger towards her.

Something was broken that cannot be repaired, a trust that stood the test of 23 years is over and what makes me angry is the selfishness that has torn a family apart and affected 5 kids. I feel betrayed by someone who I considered a friend, someone who came into my home and broke something sacred and continued as if all was ok.

As for Heather, yes it is forever over, the papers are signed and there is no chance of reconciliation. The manner in which it was done and the manner in which I found out hurt more deeply than the realization that our marriage was over. It happened in our home under our roof. Yes I am angry and frustrated that I did not see it coming, I was warned and I ignored the signs, I am angry with myself.

There a typical hiveld thunderstorm raging outside and it so reminds me of my current life. I go from complete calm and functionality to extreme frustration which I would assume borders on anger. I go from peaceful contentment to moody loneliness and dwell on what if's and if only's, this I am sure is a form of self pity as well, but I could not be bothered at present.

I am in a much better place than I was last week, yet I have such a long road ahead and desperately need my friends, all of them and I realize that I might lose some along the way. I am able to pray at last and even though they are only short prayers it is communication. I am already so different to the old Ted and yet the journey is young and many calluses and bruises await me as I stumble, run, and sometimes crawl ahead. I am learning to listen and shut up, I am learning that some people do not want you to fix things, they just want a sympathetic ear. I want to help, but I need so much help myself. I need to become more humble and accept gifts of friendship, love, advice and hospitality.

To move forward I have to face anger and I have no idea how to do that, it is easier to ignore, but no growth comes from that. I desire growth I desire movement forward and I need to realize that it doesn't mean a damn what I want, it is what God will do in His time at His pace and I have no choice, but to let God.

As for dating, that is not an option at all, company is possible but to do that in a safe environment. I definitely want to do the divorce workshop in February and this will not only help me deal with issues relating to my recovery but enable me to hopefully meet people in a safe environment.

It would be easier to meet someone anyone and just get on with a new relationship, but that would not help me now and is not what I want. Honestly, all I want now is friendship, a companion that would be happy to be a friend and a partner to do normal things with. Sigh, it sounds so simple

I am enjoying the peace and quiet and yet missing the company of my girls and friends, just can't make me happy.

So I do have mini goals in place and they include health, exercise, being a caring Dad who is always there for his girls and is consistent in his love of Jesus and keeps that as a constant in our relationship. We pray together and God willing we will be back in church soon. Also make a decision about accommodation, about work for next year and be happy at Christmas. I would also like to cook dinner for lots of people once a month. I want music and dance and clowns and midgets... sorry got a little carried away there.

Mid long term is my financial situation, the consequences thereof and the implications that will follow. I would like to go for some dinner engagements and see how that works out.

Enough for tonight...

Subject: Divorce Care

So I went to the Divorce Care 'How to cope with the Holidays' course tonight and came away from it with the following conclusions;

1. Women REALLY express their anger
2. Divorced folk can be extremely bitter
3. When you are the only male in a group of 7, you want to be the first to leave, you might not be the enemy but you do not want to take a chance either lol
4. I am totally unprepared for Christmas
5. I am very nervous, no make that scared senseless about Christmas and this is despite the fact that I have my girls with me
6. I am not sure if I can make the Christmas Day Service and pull it off or keep it together
7. I have not even thought until today about sending out Christmas Cards
8. I cannot help thinking that running away is a good option at the moment
9. The road ahead is long and involves a lot of uphill's.

Tonight I feel inadequate in so many ways, as a father, as a friend, as a man. I feel lonely and vulnerable and really not happy. The course brought home again the harsh realities of divorce, the hurt, the anger, the pain and most of all the destruction of good memories. I feel sad tonight and feel like a good cry.

My heart breaks for the pain my girls are experiencing, I want to hold them, but have to live with goodnights by sms and kisses by sms. I cannot touch feel smell comfort or even go into their rooms at night and just look at them sleeping. That is no longer an option, it is as if a thief has wandered into my soul and taken something so precious and destroyed it before my eyes. It is gone.

Goodnight my friends...

Wilderness
A conversation between 2 friends

Hello Brain,

Firstly, excellent sermon and thank you for sharing it with me, it certainly has huge similarities with my own life presently.

Secondly, if I am to spend 40 yrs in the wilderness, I will be 84 and not much use to anyone after that. lol

I am so conscious of letting go and letting God and the way He is changing me is alarming to say the least. I am completely out of my comfort zone and not sure of what each day holds. I often finish a day bruised tired and just wanting to sleep and cannot wait for the sleeping pill to kick in and just drag me off to a quiet place where nothing matters. My cynical psychopath explained to me that I do not have deep depression as I am able to get up and function in the morning, so there are little blessings along the way.

My girls are truly excited to see me and their joy is not an act, we spend a lot of time laughing together. I am both deeply saddened and yet glad and blessed beyond all recognition. No words can describe the joy and sadness that fills me when I watch my girls sleep. I just want to take them in my arms and hold them forever. Now you have made me cry.

I am aware that God uses all and in some cases disaster is required to bring about change in some stubborn peoples lives. I believe that being a natural leader like yourself, we often can be tempted to push on through on our own steam and efforts and it can be so easy to lose focus and do life. God is changing all of that in my life. I cannot keep fixing things in other peoples lives when mine is collapsing and crumbling about me.

I am angry with Heather for many things, but have to be careful not to judge her as she needs prayer and love as opposed to judgment and damnation, this I honestly feel is how the Lord has helped me to accept what has happened and slowly and I do mean slowly move along.

I cannot face Deon yet, I have not managed to open that box and this I realize is hindering my progress, I will have to do something about it soon and do not have a clue as to what when or how. Please pray for wisdom and discernment.

As for Christmas, I am dreading it and if it were not for my girls I would gladly take 2 sleeping pills and simply sleep for at least 24 hrs, this is why I believe God has sent my 2 angels to keep me company during this period. It is going to be the hardest thing I have ever done and I can honestly say that I am scared. I pray for a calming of emotions and the love of Christ to wrap me in a blanket and just smother me the whole day. I need to do it, but at the same time I do not have the strength for it. Sigh, more tears.

I have 2 wonderful male friends who will be meeting with me weekly to pray and chat and help me learn to pray or open the dialogue between God and I again, I asked for their assistance as I need to continually humble myself and realize that this journey requires me to ask for and be able to accept unconditionally, it is very hard and I am still hugely uncomfortable with it.

My angels are growing up so fast and I need to enjoy these precious times, I am envious that Heather has so much more time with them and am praying she spends it wisely, Simon is stirring and I await her first smile and my morning hug, Nicole is still out and as precious as ever, if she could wear her gold high heels to bed I am pretty sure she would.

Love you my friend,

Ted

You, Your Prostate, and Other Nasty Experiences

A visit to the Dr and a full medical and when men reach middle age we ALL know what that means. For the uninformed, the sound of a rubber glove snapping into place followed by those oh so soothing reassuring phrases; 'Just relax' or even better the no warning 'HEY I AM NOT A PUPPET.' Yes, it is about as much fun as finding Grannies false teeth in the bottom of your tea. But here is the good news lads, they can now test it by means of a simple blood test. No more fetal positions, no more sobbing afterwards and no need to devour baked beans the night before for a little revenge, nope technology has saved our butts for use of an appropriate phrase. On a more serious note, all is well except bp is a little high but sugar cholesterol liver all good. The girls and I had a really good weekend and managed to get a lot of visits in, managed to get Christmas cards sorted and Simon got her makeover and she loves it. Apparently the boys at school cannot stop staring and gossiping about it, I will need a bigger baseball bat me thinks. Nicole has a bit of a sore throat but is ok otherwise. Friday Heather is going to court for the divorce so on Friday we should officially be divorced. But lets not chat about that now. I have my last session with the cynical psychopath for the year tomorrow and then cold turkey :) Work is ongoing and I pray next year is better as this year was not a financial success. I find Monday evenings a little lonely especially after I have had the girls for a weekend but it is something that I am learning to cope with and God willing it will become easier with time.

That is all for now, time to work...

The Day Before...

I have just watched hail, well I had to start the mail somewhere and I was getting a little bored with HELLO EVERYBODY, haha.

So I saw my angels for about an hour and a half today and it was lovely, leaving was not easy and never normally is. I phoned a friend after leaving and that helped, thanks Candy.

It is so amazing that a friendly rational voice can just put all in perspective and lift a spirit that is slightly down.

It has not been a bad week, I have a prayer partner and yes I prayed aloud for the first time in a long time and meant it, it was not really a conversation but a start and for that I am grateful. I have noticed that God is not always a loud clear booming voice, sometimes it is a smile and a wave from a child at Sunday School, sometimes a hug from a male friend who does not know what to say to you, a sense of peace as you stroll on a church property, a simple sms that says 'How are you'. God uses his children to touch and reach out to us. He never gives up on us no matter how difficult and hard headed the route we take, He simply slips in beside us and is there no matter what, I am so grateful He does not give up and forgives and forgets so easily, Praise You and Thank You!

Tomorrow I am officially divorced, here's how God has such a good sense of humour, tomorrow Jan, who is Deon's wife who is now Heather's boyfriend (Hey I have my own soap opera) is also getting divorced. So the chance that they will bump into each other at court is very likely. God's timing is not for the faint hearted lol.

It has been said that I have the body of 2 x 22 year olds and apparently one of them wants their body back, so next week we crank up the old exercise routine and work towards a body fit for a speedo but not permitted in one for the sake of eternal embarrassment and shame of my angels. I have threatened to fetch the girls from school in a speedo, with gold high heels and a cape round my neck if they were not careful. I cannot describe the absolute look of terror that crossed their faces, you would think I had sacrificed fluffy puppies and made a hat from their coats.

It is not easy being a single Dad, but I have found that I am getting to like the Ted that God is slowly molding and I am no longer afraid to spend time with myself. There is a peace that comes from silence, a release of tension and a time to heal, a time to think, a time to plan and a time to appreciate the simpler things in life.

I had a haircut on Tuesday, my first in about 4 years or more, the hairdresser did ask what I wanted done, well it is still pretty short you see and I told her to take some off the top and leave the back - only kidding just wanted to type that :)

She just tidied it up a little and charged me half price; only took about 4 minutes. I can almost run my fingers through my hair, well maybe another 3 months or so and I will be able to stand on the front end of a ship about to sink and sing Celine Dion songs with my curly locks waving in the breeze, errr that sounds familiar mmmmmm

I will now leave before my imagination really gets carried away.

Love you...

Roses

Roses are Red
Violets are Blue
Hi I'm Ted and single
How about you?

It seems an appropriate way to begin, as of the 11th of December 2009, I am now legally and rightfully divorced, single, unmarried, for the first time in 23 years I do not have a partner, someone to call to love to hold to wake up next to.

Yes this does seem like a bit of déjà vu, I have written this somewhere in the past, the difference now is that it is finalized, signed stamped and sealed. The contract is undone, "till death us do part" has been replaced by "I grant this decree of divorce dated and signed today by me"

It still came as a shock even though it has been in the pipeline for a while, where did it hit home? I got invited to join a family for supper and even though I was feeling miserable and sorry for myself, I so desperately did not want to be alone that I even contemplated stopping in at a pub on the way back to the flat, but managed to restrain myself. So I received the sms to come through and jumped at it, the drive was not fun, I remembered the good times with Heather and my girls, I remembered the first few times we dated, I remembered telling my girls that we were getting divorced and the tears that followed, I considered all the times ahead without my angels, waking up alone and to silence and I cried.

Supper was lovely and I managed to laugh joke and smile and feel deeply sad at the same time, my friends were sensitive to my emotions and for that—thank you and bless you.

I came home and instead of taking a half a sleeping pill I took a full one. Did it make any difference? I still awoke before 5 so no, no difference but a new day has dawned and so it must be embraced and faced.

Please do not despair, I am not in a state of uncontrollable falling depression, I am simply sad and lonely. I realize that I am a work in progress and God is the maker and molder and my emotional state is cleansing and enables me to process and deal with issues past, present and hopefully better approach the future. I dream of having coffee in non threatening situations with friends, so if any of you are free, I need the practice and would love to buy you a cup, and yes you may opt for a herbal tea or a glass of wine, it is the company I crave.

I choose a simpler life, I choose good friends, I choose to love my girls unconditionally, I choose life and all it's aches and pains and defects but also its energy love excitement and passion. I choose happiness and realize that this is a 2 sided coin with sadness as its opposite. I choose conversations, holding hands, hugs and smiles. I choose God and have put Him in control of all the above.

Does this make it all easy and resolved, no in fact it make it harder and more painful, I have to deal with the past and its consequences and mistakes and learn and embrace the future.

From Wednesday I will have Simon and Nicole and relish having them in my life for almost 3 weeks, it is the only Christmas gift I require. I can't wait to chat laugh cuddle dance sing and maybe even play pool with Simon. :-)

For now Saturday and Sunday loom ahead and these must be dealt with.

Enjoy the Weekend...

16 December 2009

A public holiday and a new home
Another blessing for I am not alone
I pray for rest and peaceful sleep
And hope I don't end up counting sheep

I am in the most stunning house in Thornhill, lovely pool, beautiful big pub, stunning kitchen and 2 large plasma screens that seem to follow you around the lounge and entertainment area. Did I mention the pool table, well yup managed to beat myself but it was a close game.

There is a peace that seems to fill this home and I am feeling reasonably relaxed and could almost unwind here, what I am in fact saying is that I have had no curve balls today and a wonderful time with my girls.

I am doing a lot of thinking and at times I can feel myself slipping into a downward spiral but then words of encouragement get sent to me, thank you. You have no idea what a relief and blessing they have been and as usual the timing has been perfect. God is still molding me and I feel that the most drastic changes are and have been occurring in the last month, I can almost feel the tugging at my soul sometimes on a daily if not an hourly basis. As the old Ted tries to take control again, I can feel the inner battle of will vs Spirit and it is these times that leave me sensitive and vulnerable, there are still so many raw nerve endings, I almost believed that the whole process was nearing an end. In fact my journey is still very new and there is so much I need to be taught and re-taught that I must confess that I geared myself for a sprint where in fact a marathon is required.

If this is to be the case, I need to refocus and adjust MY expectations and let God in fact continue the job I have agreed to, you see God is going to do it whether I let Him or not because for so long I have been doing it MY way and where has that got me? Into a hell of a lot of trouble, in a sewerage farm without nose plugs!

I have new challenges awaiting me come the new year and these need to be addressed now, accommodation is of the utmost importance. My mail order bride required proof of residence and Deanne has refused to allow me to have her delivered to her home, something about teenage boys and Brian smiling too much, lol But seriously, I need to put some roots down, a foundation, somewhere I can collect my goodies and create a home that will allow me to show my girls the sort of stability they are seriously lacking presently.

Hand in hand with my search for proof of residence is some stability in our industry so that I can afford this home and address the other demon that awaits me in 2010, debt! I do sincerely believe that 2010 will be a good year and that God will not only change me, but also give me a new lease on life, a second chance, a new home, an opportunity to cement my relationship with my girls, strengthen the bonds with my incredible group of old friends and amazing new friends. For me to be able to be used I have to become humble, I need to learn to receive openly and graciously and trust God in all I do. This is easier said than done and for this I will need your prayers, sms's, conversations and friendship. Sometimes I call you not because I have something to say, just to hear a friendly voice to calm my thoughts and reclaim a little sanity. If the conversation has lull's or you find yourself wondering what the heck that was all about, please know you have blessed me just by being at the other end of a phone. I would prefer to kidnap you one at a time and have you on hand for these conversations, but our new constitution forbids this as it apparently infringes on people's rights (a mere technicality) but one I shall not pursue so rest easy.

Simonne is growing up so quickly and her move to High School next year is yet another milestone, she is such a blessing but is battling with many issues and wresting with emotions and anger and still trying to keep a happy face through it all. She has a lot of my temperament and tends to bottle up so much, however the anger is seeping out and she faces a tough couple of months. Nicole is very similar to Heather and tends to explode and then calm down and move on as well, she also cries easier than my Simon and this allows a release of emotions.

Please pray for my girls and for wisdom, discernment and sensitivity in dealing with them and the challenges they face. New schools, new friends, new home, new situation at home, a lot for them to deal with.

Heather has decided that she cannot afford to keep our house and as such it will be going on the market very soon, this of course also means that the girls will be moving once the sale is through so more drama and emotions to face.

On that note, let me bid you a good night and till we chat again...

20 December 2009

The Week that was...

It is Sunday night and another week has passed and I am once again facing the prospect of a new week, with new challenges, new situations that will require radical emotional mood ups and downs. Christmas is coming and I have no idea of the emotions that will be stirred, awaken, shaken in my soul.

I have my girls and they soak up so much of my time that it is a blessing as I have been doing less thinking and more sleeping. I am sleeping like a man dead to the world and then waking and passing out again. I am not sure if it a state of relaxation because of the new accommodation, exhaustion from the heat and the end of a year, some kind of response to the divorce, who knows. I feel drained and weary by night time and pass out, yes I still require the sleeping pills to begin the process.

My girls are awesome and we had a really good chat today, there is so much anger from them, so many fears and concerns about next year, accommodation, needs, frustration and broken promises. My heart cries out for them and I have to reassure myself that I can only do what I promised and be the best Dad possible. It is not easy when you are still trying to get it all together yourself. I have to find someone for them to talk to next year as they have many issues to resolve and work through, as I have begun to work through mine so they too need to be given the same opportunity. We all sleep in one room in a 3 bedroom home, why because they want to be near me and just love being together, this is not possible at their home anymore.

I have had enough of this year, it has been a year of sadness, difficulty, hardship and destruction and at the same time new opportunities, new and old friendships, love and unbelievable generosity and restoring my relationship with God. We have been blessed by love, prayers, affection and food for the holidays. Bless you all, you have no idea what a blessing you have all been to us.

I have started discovering the old Ted again. It not a process I am happy with as I am not in control.

I look forward to next year, I need a new start, a new beginning, a new home and who knows what else it has in store for me. I am a little scared to guess so let's see what comes along and we can share in the new adventure.

I attended the evening service with my girls tonight and it was ok, a good sermon, but could not partake in communion. Baby steps.

Emotionally I am ok, well not great, but keeping it together. I feel fragile at times and other times confused and also overwhelmed by all that has happened and the speed with which it has happened.

I feel I am waffling so goodnight and till later...

He Offers Hope

He offers Hope . . .

If I am a body my girls are my one of my lungs, I am able to function without one, however my capacity to live life fully is limited, my ability to perform optimally is reduced, I am in effect a vehicle running on 2 cylinders, a sprinter recovering from an injury, a blind man in a strange environment.

I am currently rethinking the sermon from Sunday, it dealt with pride and made me realize that I am in fact so in need of my Saviour and His grace that it is only by His awesome love that I am able to even consider any form of recovery. I have no right to any of this so called worldly justice and retribution, God is my refuge and I need to recover under His amazing love, I need to draw closer to Him and renounce this pull, this seductive lure of humanity and sin. I am a sinner. I am a man who has fallen so low that it is only Jesus that has been able to lift my head, look me in the eyes and say, "Ted, you're ok and I love you as you are!"

Man o man, how does anybody say that? How can anyone look through my transgressions, mistakes and brokenness and then still smile and say, "I love you"? After I have let him down as a father, husband, spiritually slapped Him in the face and turned my back on Him and STILL He smiles and welcomes me back with open arms and unconditional forgiveness. It is grace. I do not deserve this, I have not earned this, I am blessed out of my socks and my God Rocks.

He is my friend, my Father, my Saviour, He is the friendly face in a hostile crowd, He is the arm around my shoulders when I am sobbing, He is the hand on the steering wheel when I am unable to see the road, He is the silent partner next to me when I am alone and feeling sorry for myself, He is not just not just my God, He is my friend and He loves me warts and all.

For all the times I have come across as arrogant, uncaring, a bull in a teacup, I apologise most sincerely, for all the words I have spoken in careless disregard for any of you, I ask your forgiveness, for insensitivity in times of need, sorry. I am learning that all that is spoken has a profound effect on all around and all that is not spoken in love is in fact able to destroy and break down. Again my apologies.

For me to be the man God wants, the Father my girls deserve, the friend that can be relied on, the godfather who will be of use I need to in a relationship with God that enables me to trust and obey, for this to be true I must lay aside what is the old Ted and welcome the new. The change that has begun within must continue and I cannot smother the workings of the Holy Spirit, however painful and uncomfortable it may be.

I must stop drowning and begin to swim, I can do all things through my God and I have to use that as my lifeline and believe it.

This is a daily task and so I must rise and greet the day like an old friend and trust that Jesus is my shadow, always there, not always vocal, but never far from me.

25 December 2009

I feel the anger throbbing through my veins, pumping like pistons in an engine building up compression, I have no way of releasing the tension, It is swelling in my chest like a tyre that is overinflated. I am tired.

It was a difficult day, sad and distant.

I lay on a floor staring at the ceiling thinking of Christmas last year and felt sad, I remembered and I felt sad. I was hugged by Simon and she asked me what was wrong, you can't fool kids. They see through all our bullshit.

This evening I lay on a trampoline and stared at clouds and half a moon, pretty symbolic, the clouds were not moving and the moon looked really lonely distant almost heart broken

Simon told me that she enjoyed this Christmas more than last year.

I watched my angels opening their presents and wished I could freeze that moment and imprint on my heart forever.

I want to run away but who will care for my angels I want to hide till next year but must smile and act normal I want to be alone but cannot be.

If I had one wish what would it be; Happiness, Inner Peace, Love, Someone Special... I don't know. If I was granted a wish I would not know what to wish for, I don't know what to wish for BESIDES my girls being happy and safe that is all I wish for.

The road to recovery is a steep uphill and I often have to crawl and I feel as if my palms and knees are bleeding, I continue and sometimes I can walk and sometimes I rest.

Tonight I am unable to walk or crawl so I write

I write so that I am able to say goodnight
I write in the hope to see the light
I write so love will find a way
Back in my heart oh God I pray
I write to fight off demons with eyes tight shut
And often wonder if I am just another nut
I write so my heart will mend
I write because it is not yet the end
I write to make the tears worthwhile
I write because I want to smile
I write because it will someday make sense
And until then I trust in my friends

Goodnight...

Subject: 4 January 2010

I have been tossing and turning, attempting to fall asleep since 2 and to no avail. The sleeping tablet cannot assist me tonight, my mind is racing with all that has occurred, is happening and needs to be put into place in my life.

This is the end of a wonderful 3 weeks with Simon and Nicole and it has been a blessing beyond words. I am saddened for the loneliness that awaits me on their departure and the ordeals that they must in turn face without me. I realise that they will get through this as I will, but also am in tune with the reality that the road ahead is still long.

I am deeply angered and can feel that I have been grinding my teeth in my sleep as I deal with emotional situations and comments that my girls should not have to be subjected to. There are boundaries, rules that need to be put in place and I am praying that Heather and I will be able to put our differences aside and discuss this maturely. Nicole tells me that she battles to sleep at home yet these 3 weeks she has slept like a baby with hardly any bouts of nauseousness. My Simon is battling with invasion of her privacy and intense anger and is using her new Goth look to express some of this, for all of this she still melts in my arms when we hug or wrestle. Nicole just wants quality time and sometimes this is just sitting next to her while she watches tv. She tells me that she misses her cuddles with Mom and my heart angers and breaks for her.

I took most of the girls clothing back yesterday as they had brought enough to effectively move in :) and while they were taking it inside to their rooms, I spent some real quality time with Lucy my boerboel and she was so happy and excited to see me. Life is not easy.

I believe that I have found the appropriate accommodation, however I am only able to view it on the 11th of Jan, I am seeing another flat later today. Accommodation has become one of my major concerns and I am desperate to put this behind me so that I am able to focus on other pressing matters.

The home we have been housesitting has been such a blessing and this ends tomorrow. God is in control I keep telling myself, at times willing myself to believe it when doubt begins to creep in.

Christmas was spent with wonderful friends who as usual opened their home and hearts to me and my girls, thank you and bless you. New Year was the same and when I hit emotional low points on both I could pull aside and withdraw. To my special friends that helped me through this and dragged me back on the dance floor to the shouts of Gloria Gaynor's *I will Survive*, you guys rock!!!

As for News Year's resolutions, they are simple: move ahead, let God and never give up.

It is now closer to 4 in the morning and I will attempt some much needed sleep.

Good morning world and God Bless...

Fly Away

Have you ever felt like running away or just curling up and dying? I feel as if there is a pillow being forced down on my face and I am struggling to breathe.

On top of that I have offended and hurt some very close friends and even though I have apologised I feel really really crappy about it all. Worse is that it was not intentional and at the time I did not even realise I was doing it.

I just want to fill my lungs with air and shout and reach for the heavens, the Lenny Krawitz song with the words 'I want to fly away I want to fly away yeah yeah' keep going through my head.

I need to get out of Jhb for a night or so to try and clear my head and attempt to focus and gather my thoughts.

Hello Kim,

Thanks for the mail and the kind words. It has been a horrible week and on Friday I felt so low that if I had a couple of thousand cash and a bike I would have disappeared. I was happy to die and just leave all of this behind me, sigh but a new week starts tomorrow.

I am between a home at the moment with enough clean clothes for a week but not ironed. I am looking at a batchelor flat tomorrow that will God willing be my new home. I NEED a home Kim, this limbo state I find myself in is soul destroying and I have just closed up emotionally and I so badly need to just cry and let it all out. The problem is I have no safe haven to do it in so I just bottle it all up.

I spent 2 nights in Pretoria with my sister but that didn't help much it was good to see her though.

Thanks Kim and love to Dave...

7 to 17 Jan

There is an old couple sitting opposite me staring out of the window, it a tactic they seem to have employed to prevent themselves from speaking to each other.

What makes us stop talking to each other? Is it the pace of the rat race we call life? Is it an act of selfishness and loss of compassion for each other?

Has society made this acceptable?

We live our lives at such a pace that it is not easy to slow down, breathe in and almost view our surrounding in slow motion. We might actually be able to enjoy where we are and who we are with.

So much has happened and I have gone from a state of horrible deep depression to unbelief and wonder and amazement. Our God is so awesome and so wonderful that words cannot describe His wonderful timing love and blessings. I went from sitting in a car park considering running away to my so called 25 hours of miracles. In 25 hours I had a flat and Nicole in a brilliant school 50m from my new flat and about 80m from brilliant friends that have become family to the girls and I.

Nicole absolutely adores her school and can't stop thanking me, I explained to her that it was God and not me that made it all possible.

On Saturday we moved in and again Shane and his son Daniel jumped in with a bakkie and trailer, Deanne, Candy and Simon cleaned like women possessed, Travis carried till he almost passed out and Brian ran all over town collecting and keeping us in food and drink. You guys all rock harder than AC/DC! Nicole even with her tooth acting up again was brilliant. Wayne and Cher bless you for putting up with me in your home and allowing my angels in on Friday night.

My flat looks amazing, my girls spent the weekend with me and love their new home!

And so a new chapter begins and with God leading the way I will take a deep breathe and step out to meet this week head on.

I don't want to get to 60 and realise that life has slipped me by, I do not want to be the old couple sitting in a coffee shop ignoring each other and looking so bored with life.

Bless you all for your prayers, thoughts, encouragement and assistance...

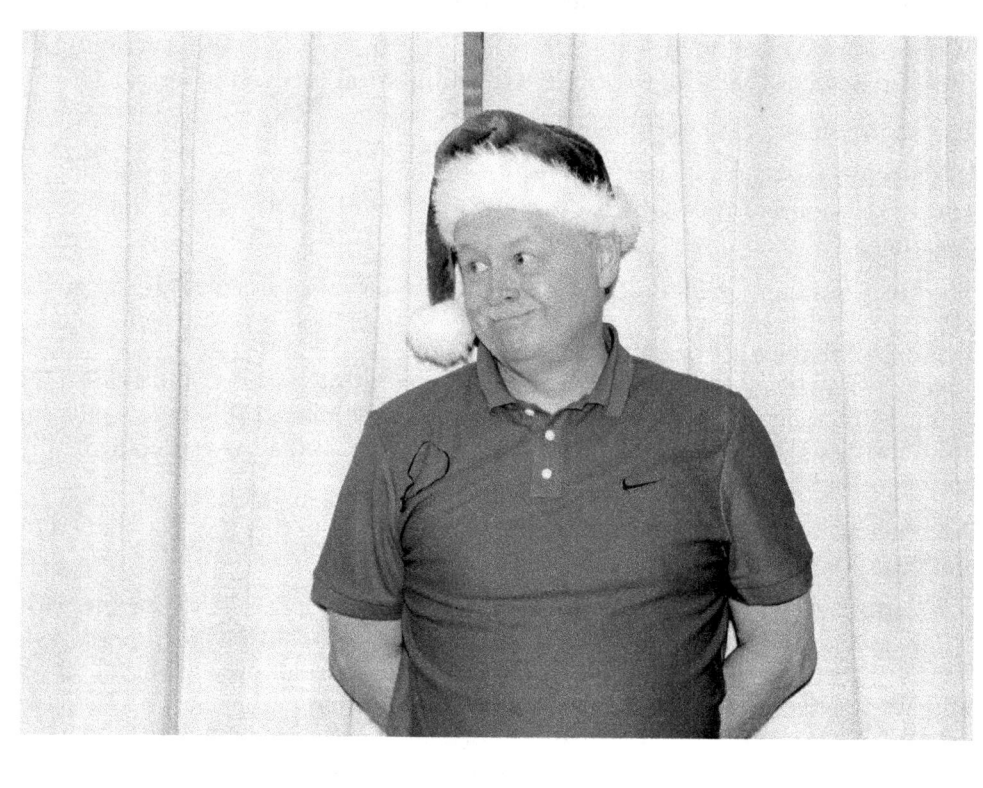

Subject: Parental Advisory Warning

I awoke to a stunning morning and tempted to give Heather a couple of missed calls and then after I stopped smiling I made myself a really good mug of Ethiopian coffee. Back in bed and decided whether to cry, sneak up on my shadow or try and fit my hand into a lamp shade hole so small I would have to break it to get it out. So in sheer desperation I simply went to the kitchen and glared at the sweet jar and rearranged my coffee in the fridge.

I discovered that no matter how many people like tea, at 23h15 you are drinking alone!

Better read the next section with one eye closed!

I danced naked in the bath this morning and wiggled my bum but refrained from shout whoooop whoooop, thought I would save that a good morning.

I am considering getting a rubber duck as a companion and bath buddy, any suggestions for a name?

Emotionally I am extremely low at the moment and the evenings really get to me, oh if only I was a vampire, I would then be able to eat out every night.

What I miss the most is someone to talk to at night!

It is amazing how much we take for granted when we "have" it all. I am still tempted to run away from it all, but I know I have to stop and ask myself what would Scooby Doo?

Well the weekend is now officially here so enjoy, love you all...

February's Coming

It has not been a fun 2 weeks.

I have been really battling and the evenings have been absolute torture. What has also been such a knockout blow is when the realisation dawned that this life experience is not a sprint, but in fact a marathon. I have put so much energy into the sprint that when I reached the top of the proverbial finish line on that hill of hell, all I saw were more valleys and no finish line anywhere in site.

How do you run a race when you don't have a finish line? How do you pace yourself? How can you focus on the future when the present is beating you black and blue?

Does this mean that there have been no blessings, no love, no hope? No, in fact the complete opposite is true, my girls and I have been blessed out of our socks and I cannot thank you all enough for the blessings and prayers. Bless each and every one of you!

I am still battling to sleep without medication, no let me rephrase that, I CANNOT sleep without medication. I can't pray because whenever I close my eyes and try and focus on hearing God the noise and chaos in my head drowns out any chance of that. So how do you hear His voice when there is no peace except when you have been knocked out at night?

My cynical psychopath agreed that a friends suggestion that a written short prayer is a brilliant idea. Thank you! She also suggested lighting a candle at night to help focus on my girls and just to remind me of the reasons to carry on with this voyage of recovery. So I bought 2 scented candles and that posed an immediate problem, they are covered in plastic, are you supposed to remove the plastic or is it the burny type? Help!

Right now Simon is fast asleep next to me and I received the most beautiful smiles and hugs from her, they are so precious and I love my girls so much.

Please take the time to constantly look around you and appreciate all and especially those who mean something to you, when it has been taken away it is too late. I am learning that time and special moments pass so quickly and once an opportunity is gone it can not be rewound.

There is also so much guilt I am dealing with and Regan and I really went into it on Thursday, please just pray for wisdom and forgiveness on my part.

Enough for now and till next time...

Lesotho Nights

Africa Beckons

The truth of the matter is that I was not coping, I had no sports car, no penthouse suite and my flats contents consisted of gifts from my parents and friends who had bent over backwards to assist me in providing a livable home for my girls and I.

I was behind on everything, school fees, bills that kept me awake at night and calls from unknown numbers that I did not answer. When people called and asked if I was Ted Lodewijks, I would enquire who they were and where they were calling from before I confirmed that I was indeed him or simply hung up the phone.

I was not running away because I had nowhere to go to and no idea of how to pay to get there.

Hence, at very short notice I was offered a job away from home for 18 months in another country. After discussing it with my girls we agreed that I should go.

It is a huge step to walk away from your two teenage daughters and leave in the care of someone you no longer love or respect.

The African Adventure Begins

Imagine a land of gumboots, umbrellas, donkeys, upside down wheelbarrows, blanket people and medium sized rocks on your house roof. A place where all Europeans are referred to as Chinese in the rural areas and English is often greeted with a look of confusion, similar to the look my boerboel Lucy used to give me if I didn't bring her a McDonald's cheeseburger back from town.

It is a smog free country with night skies so clear you can see stars that haven't even made their debut in the cities yet, a truly magnificent African display of constellations.

Also present are a collection of tired, semi-disabled vehicles, some resting and adorning a greenery where the engine used to be and others waiting for a transplant in an donor-less environment.

The folk are friendly and patient and more importantly content with a simple lifestyle. there is a younger generation bursting through with the enthusiasm of puppy attacking a toilet roll and they are keen to get out and get to Johannesburg. They want the things they see on television and the rock and roll lifestyle. I am hoping this remains the dream of the kids in the city and that the rural folk remain pure, holistic and culturally rich.

Winter has not yet graced us with her presence, I am told she is bitter, wicked and has an ice cold heart. It will definitely snow and for us South Africans who think that a temperature of 21'C is a little cool, I expect to hear the clinking of frozen balls as I walk.

It is time to leave for now and until we meet again, let me grace you with this word of wisdom, "Close the fridge door, I'm freezing"

Nite All...

African Month

Life in Lesotho can best be described as trading in the Johannesburg highways with its aggressive drivers and slowing it all down to slow motion, similar to the now infamous Pamela Anderson Baywatch jogging scene in her airbrushed bikini.

It is relaxed. People chat to you and because my skin is of a paler complexion, I am no longer referred to as "Chinese" but am now American. I am only partially convinced that this nothing to do with me being twice the size of the average Chinese, however bulk is seen as an asset here.

We have started our vegetable garden and our gardener speaks next to no English, hence we both smile a lot at each other and I have no idea what he has planted where. My sign language is a combination of hand signals with some body movement, basically I look like a chubby version of Michael Jackson doing a moonwalk without moving my feet.

Work is currently 90% admin and 10% site work, I sometimes feel like a school teacher who never gets the apple. Our accommodation is compact but clean and serviced daily, food is good although I never thought I would say, but the amount of red meat we consume is enough to make the mildest of vegetarians refer to us as cannibalistic murderers. This I am led to believe is not a compliment.

When we feel the walls of our rooms getting a little close and the sudden urge to hug our male colleagues, we head off to Maseru and grab a meal and a movie. The owner of the local Spur never leaves us alone and all the waiters apologise if someone is sitting in our table, and what do we order? CHICKEN!

So in short, it is a beautiful country with the most brilliant stars at night, friendly people and a pace of life which explains why the donkey is the transport vehicle of choice.

Nite All...

Frosty Bits

I am cold, colder than the heart of a divorce lawyer or a cat who is ignoring you.

There was snow and I am not in favour of it. It is just a pre-requisite for mud and has the potential of ice on steps. Now this led to a knock on my door at 21h00 on Saturday night as one of my work colleagues fell up a flight of stairs. After pointing and an initial spurt of acceptable mocking, I did what any neighbour would do, I gave him 4 Disney character plasters. The look of utter disgust was priceless and I had to stop myself from giving him a peck on the cheek.

Life on site has entered a routine and the advent of a week of sub-zero temperatures and snow has certainly cast a little disconcertment amongst us all, almost like a huge rump steak in the company of vegetarians. Please don't get me wrong, I once knew of a girl who heard a tale of her distant aunt's twin daughter-in-laws roommate who bumped into a vegetarian at an anti-prenuptial rally in some distant American State.

I bought a pair of longjohns this weekend and am now in need of thermal underwear before it reaches the stage where a vasectomy is no longer required and I will be left with nothing to scratch when I awaken in the morning. Pre-waking needs for bladder visits to the loo have now become instances of dash and slash with the acute possibility of a splash.

So into the cold frosty yonder I venture until we next cross paths

Nite All...

Rural Bathing

Two days without bathing and I feel as if I am on the verge of launching a new kind of body odour called "You're Feisty".

Our water is pumped up to a holding tank and then distributed as and when we require it, when we have a power outage, we have no water and the odour of the past creeps back like heartburn after a dodgy pie.

I had set aside 3 wetwipes from a restaurant chain and this would been my plan of attack if the electric gods once again felt us unworthy of their gifts. It's moments like these that make living in Africa great, we have so much we take for granted and yet we have this fickle structure that is as reliable as Blackberry's future.

I awoke and water ran from the tap and I had to fight down the urge to run down the passageway singing "Rock and Roll dreams come true". It was a beautiful moment and even though the water pressure was a weak as a priests alibi on a youth camp, it was enough for me to wash all the bits that needed attending to.

So here I am at my desk, sick as a dog with flu, but not smelling like a lemon scented wetwipe and grateful for running water and electricity.

Nite All...

Gypsy Anyone?

It is very easy to get caught up in the business of "Woe is me" and the world is out to get me, it is a scenario of not being your fault or being within my ability to change it.

When I was down and hating the world, I battled to get out of bed, out of my flat and out to visit my friends. It was easier to hide away and wallow in the darkness of my soul and room.

There is certainly a time for this and it was a time to reflect, heal and re-assess what I expected and wanted from life. I also used this time to analyze and dissect family and friends in my mind and place them in the boxes I had created. I file with my mind and am thus able to open and explore when I wish and also bury and hide other chapters till I am strong enough to open them.

So what is the purpose of this blog?

I don't know yet, bear with me and I ramble on. Oh wow rambles, remember when we had Arts & Crafts Rambles, people dressed like hippies and use words like "organic" "cosmic" "earthy" "karma" and could all be used in a sentence to like totally numb my colon. I loved that environment, people worked with their hands and had a wandering community of friends, yes there were politics but how serious could it be with a cosmic organic karma and vegetarian crafter who made leather bags and shoes.

So you can either hide and drown in your life or else throw a little caution to the wind and maybe live a little. I am not saying sell everything and start knitting your own underwear while you hug strawberries and French beans. Maybe just re-evaluate where you are in your life, decide if it has been a worthy life and if you are ready for an adventure, start with a little one.

I left my room with the aid of some amazing friends and a Mom who spent ages on her knees praying for me. It has been fun, at times scary and with an amazing lady holding my hand, I am learning to love and be loved again.

Nite All...

Rent a Midget

I am cold, freezing and in need of a hot water bottle or a midget to use to warm me. The Queen of Hearts in Alice in Wonderland had the right idea of using a warm pigs belly to rest her feet on, bravo evil Queen bravo.

It was -6° C last night and we had no water or electrical appliances due to our power board lighting up like a terrorist touring an explosive factory and then it died, tragically. Dark descended and with it came its extremely unpopular sidekick, Cold.

I was in bed by 7 and asleep by 8 complete with my thermal socks and only my eyes peeping out from beneath the blankets, I awoke at 02h00 and was cold. This is the first time since I have been in Lesotho that I have been cold at night, hence my request for a midget that I can move around to warm the cold bits of my body.

If any of you have a spare midget lying around, I would be most grateful if I loan the little bugger.

If I have offended any of you with my simple request for warmth and comfort, I apologise most profusely and will allow you visitation rights to midgetville, however I must urge you not to spoil them as midget tossing and Leon Schuster movies depend on them for their livelihood.

On that emotional note, I have the following to say,

Nite All...

Spring Fever

Spring

It's when trees blossom and people seem to emerge from the sewers of winter wearing smiles and exposing white bleached skin to all and sundry.

Smiles replace grimaces and layers of clothing are replaced by tight t-shirts, amazing on the ladies but not so enduring on fully bodied middle aged men like myself. Picnics and walking and for some cycling become the order of the day as the winter kilos are frowned upon and the search for the perfect beach body commences.

I went for an half an hour brisk walk yesterday midst the locals who giggled and called me names I am sure refer to my rock and roll walking nature, red face and gasps of air. Some followed for a short while like vultures expecting me to drop and die so that they could pick me off like a corpse. I came back to my room and collapsed on my bed and dreamt of beer, cold frothy and oh so smooth, my bottled water tasted as exciting as Liverpool's Premier League survival. The need for bottled water is not due to my extravagant lifestyle, no it has to do with the chemical smell and white sizzling nature of the local water on tap. I prefer my body to rust the old fashioned way, by means of lager and pilsner.

I am always reminded of the following quote when I begin outdoor exercising, "I don't trust joggers! It's just coincidental that they are the ones that find all the dead bodies"

Avoid bushes, watches and jewelry that lurk within your reach, you will discover that they are attached to a body and that leads to valuable time away from friends and pubs giving police statements. It also keeps you from exercising if you ever venture outdoors again. Perhaps this will explain the surge in the sale of treadmills in cities.

So besides the dead bodies and hayfever, you have picnics, beach parties and braais with friends. Embrace Spring and feast on the t-shirts fellas.

Nite...

Bullies

We all have a thorn in our side, a bug who we would like to squash and strut away into the sunset sipping on a canned beverage.

Some of life's problems can be resolved by turning the other cheek, being the bigger person or smiling in the face of adversity, others however . . . . .

In the early days of divorce there are so many raw emotions and confused thoughts that you wear your emotions on your sleeve. Snapping, outbursts and overwhelming emotions with a tendency to take all comments personally don't help the situation.

It has now been close to three years that I have been divorced and friends, family and a very patient therapist have turned me into a human being, well not according to all that is. What has changed is that I have learnt to express my self, so instead of saying "That was not the most intelligent decision of your life" I might be tempted to utter "OMG did we have to flush all our brain cells away this morning? Could we not have saved 3 to keep us ahead of Neanderthal man? Really"

Being honest has helped me to stop myself from having my third stroke, so far so good.

Back to the thorny little bullies, in this case a limp wristed pencil pushing spoilt human who has no people skills and the tact of a sailor in a brothel, someone who has no management experience and uses their lack of skills to bully those below them by means of pulling "rank". Such a spineless silver spoon fed protected enema of a human specimen only understands one form of response, attack.

So I lost it, not proud of my actions, but in this case justified as it required this method of interaction to send back the slithering sloth to the hole from where it crawled.

Bullies only understand a show of force, it requires this for them to leave you be and search for an easier prey who will bow down to their little power plays.

Inner peace, meditation and calm, maybe tomorrow.

Nite All...

Hair Attack

I noticed that with maturity comes unwanted traits that I never seemed to be aware of in people before. I have aches in parts of my body caused by sport when I still thought of myself as invincible, for example if I am on the floor it requires a set of moves that would make a Chinese wrestler proud just to get back on my feet.

Another side effect or mutation is the emergence of Lone Ranger hairs.

They work alone, spring up when you least expect them and will ride against the natural direction of the other hairs. They also prefer areas where they can expose themselves to world with pride; ears, eyebrows and nostrils to name three. I was not going to be intimidated by one such hair on my eyebrow and decided to attack it with a set of tweezers, I should add that my Simon or Nicole are normally the ones that remove these outcasts of society for me.

So the battle commenced.

I lost.

I was slaughtered and for my efforts I now sported a bald spot which is not in fashion and could not be covered up. I believe the final tally was as follows, "Mad Grey Hair's removed nil and normal eyebrow hairs removed twenty".

For my last tattoo on my back, the area had to be shaved before the tattoo commenced, I have come to accept that it is a battle that I am beginning to lose. However, every now and then I arise like a phoenix and attack and pluck and shave till I am once more granted access to state acceptable to 10 years ago.

Rock & Roll Grub

It's fun, it's sensual and it's as sinful as wearing a loincloth made of bacon to a temple ceremony and you weren't even on the guest list.

Its like meeting your new date's parents and hitting on her Mom, its the orgasmic response to the first bite of a meal so good you want to cry.

Rock and roll depicts a theology and lifestyle that is more than the image of wild orgies and drugs, no my friends it is so much more than that. It's just a step to the left, and a jump to the right, its rock and roll dreams come true, its a crazy little thing to call love. Dreams then can come true, a smile and slow dance so intense that if you were to kiss, a crowbar would be required to pry you apart, yes my rocking friend, it's all about passion and living for that moment.

Rock and roll food is the same, its the juicy cheese burger complete with a slice of tomato and lettuce on a soft seeded roll, a beef patty the thickness of your thumb and hot crispy fries. As you bite into it, hot juices run down your chin and drip onto your plate, the taste of grilled beef and melted cheese awaken a stirring in you and you close your eyes and just relish the moment. It is a meal that awakens memories and if shared with a loved one you cant help but flirt with them as you lick your fingers between bites. You stroke the juices on your plate with a chip and the crunch as you bite into it sounds like ice cracking, slightly salty, hot and tainted with pleasure. Its a ballad of love found, lost and never forgotten. It's a kiss in an alley, it's sneaking under their t-shirt and their sharp intake of breath as you make contact with their skin.

The smell, the taste, the experience is what makes it the ultimate rock and roll meal. Its about falling in love all over again or getting over a crashed relationship. Accompany it with great music and you can face another day or tackle the impossible.

Nite All...

The 3rd Option

I have been away from my girls for 36 days by the time I get back to Johannesburg on Wednesday, that's a long time and add to that the lack of power, which in turn relates to a lack of water and hence no flushing toilet facilities.

Yes I can carry water up 2 flights of stairs for the toilet, but it has an odd metallic chemical taste and I fear that drinking it may lead to the spontaneous origination of a third nipple or testicle, both which pose dilemmas I do not wish to expose. There is a mental picture I carry in my head of wearing a button up shirt and stretching back as we sometimes do, and lo and behold my middle nipple popping through and scaring all in sight.

The other option is far more graphic and disturbing, picture me running... better make that walking, slowly on the beach, I become lightheaded from the over exertion and fall over onto my back, legs slightly splayed. Lifeguard rushes in to "save and resuscitate" me, and by accident notices a third lump in my speedo. The third teste phenomena was stated on the coroners docket as my cause of death.

As a matter of interest, how would you walk with a third fella down there? Would you need to seat yourself with more care in lieu of perhaps sitting on one of the three?

This my friends is what goes through my mind whenever our power dies, for the record to date I have no glowing beams emanating from any part of my body so radioactivity can be ruled out.

On that happy note

Nite All...

It Approaches

It's a wonderful time of the year, well almost. School kids are already finished with school and the first "I am sooo bored" has already made its appearance. For parents, most of us are counting the days down until we are on holiday.

I have enjoyed Lesotho immensely and yet I welcome a break from it now, I need a shower every day, I need water that I can drink and a break from fried mess hall food. Oh and the flies, the African Budgie, a beast so lazy and disgusting it pales in comparison to computer generated exes. They seem to send in wave upon wave of flying raisins and rest on all that is sacred and edible, definitely more irritating than a 2 year old throwing a tantrum in a shopping centre whilst Mommy dearest tries to reason with it. I use the term "it" because if it was any other species, the mother would do the honorable deed and eat the little beast in full public view of any other potential brats.

A month away from my girls is never easy and when I am weakened by a stomach bug, it makes the whole process a little harder. My body aches more than a 55 year old man's whose 29 year old girlfriend has lured him to yoga lesson because it will help him to reach that spiritual place when they are making love. I can't wait to hit the road with my girls, road-trip music, adventure and visiting family, this memory creator will be documented by way of blogs and photos, blank spaces filled in by fresh fruit, ice-cream and beer and as many hugs as a man could bear.

It will also be a time for me to spend with my Mom and discuss the way ahead for my Dad, a conversation I don't relish but one that must be dealt with.

It is also a time of the year where Simon, Nicole and I have been on the receiving end of friend's kindness and I am indeed overwhelmed that this generosity has been bestowed upon us, I find it difficult to respond except to say thank you.

This to me is the true spirit of these approaching holidays, sharing and laughing with loved ones. It is a time for friends and family to reflect on the past year and forget about the hard-times and just revel in that moment of happiness.

Nite All...

Black and White

So it seems that dogs see life in black and white and I was thinking that this may indeed be a wonderful way to see life for a while. Please don't assume that I am not a fan of the spectrum of colours that bless me when I stub my toe or cut myself shaving, but I often do not appreciate them with a lego block wedged in my heel.

The absence of colour assists me to focus on the object at hand, it enhances the subject and fades the additional extras into a background haze that rests like an exhausted puppy. A beautiful portrait, a wedding or a funeral can be expressed in a manner that colour cannot match. (It has been brought to my attention that the only difference between a Brakpan wedding and a Brakpan funeral is one less drunk).

Would this work in all situations? No, nature, food, and boy bands need to be encased in the full spectrum of colours.

Why boy bands?

Well to capture them in black and white would somehow somehow elevate them above the dressed, patted and painted synchronised musical monkeys they deserve, colour shows them as they truly are and entitles them their lollipop candyfloss moment of recognition.

When I am in the process of photoshopping the colour out of a picture or bleaching it, I am always amazed at the transformation and personality that the photo takes on, it transcends itself from a mere collection of millions of coloured pixels to a story begging to be shared.

Colour somehow invokes the feeling of motion and movement whereas black and white seems to stop and capture that precise moment and freeze it forever sealing it in a timeless capsule. That's what does it for me, I have that moment forever locked in a frame and encased in glass.

Click click

Nite All...

African Trimmings

I went for a haircut, at a local hairdresser and I was told a beautiful lady would be cutting my hair. As I was seated and prepped, an African lady larger than me with enough padding around her bottom to stuff a full lounge suite greeted me.

When she asked scissors or "that hair shearing thing what's name I just forgot" I should have smelt a rat, I said scissors of course, being adventurous.

Then she brought scissors and one of those big combs the blacks with Afros keep in their hair.

So I figured, this is a well setup hairdresser that charges R25 for a haircut so it should be ok? All true.

Right? Hell no.

She used the scissors and comb and proceeded to remove a huge chunk out of the right side of my head.

Some sense returned as Danny my work colleague and friend abruptly turned and walked out laughing.

I put my specs on and did I leave? No.

I told her that maybe the shearer would be better. She smiled and almost skipped off to get it.

Danny came in smiling like a bloody naughty kid, it looked like he had been crying his eyes were so wet.

She came back and asked if she should shave the top the same length as the back and Danny left the shop again. No, I stayed, not sure if it was shock or stupidity at this stage.

She used a No. 4 all over and then back came the scissors.

She did the round the ear bits and I prayed and apologised for all I had and would ever do. Returneth the crying Danny.

He asked my beautifully gifted hair stylist if she would mind if he could help AND SHE YES!!! What the hell.

He did a No. 3 round the back and sides, then asked for a No. 2. He did the edges and sides AGAIN with it and I was not saying a word. I asked how it looked and I could have sworn I heard him snort.

It was over. I got a wash AFTER the haircut AND paid full price for it.

As we walked out he laughed like a bloody idiot, the reason he had to use the No. 2 was that on the other side to the big comb cut disaster, she had cut a stripe while trimming round my ear. The No. 3 didn't remove it.

Sigh. It was a real experience for the costly sum of R25 or $2.

The moral of the story once again is that Africa is not for sissies.

Nite All...

Words

Picture yourself in a boat on a river,
With tangerine trees and marmalade skies
Somebody calls you, you answer quite slowly,
A girl with kaleidoscope eyes. —Lennon-McCartney

When you dwell in the Land of the Mountain Kingdom and have adjusted to the pace dictated by non-Western influenced society, you have the option of either venting and complaining or alternatively embracing it.

There are many factors to add to the collage that is my mind and imagination as I contemplate who I am and where I am today, a love lost, but 2 amazing daughters came from it. Retrenchment, unemployment and depression followed by grave moments of self-doubt that have brought me to where I am now, starting anew despite financial organisations that seek the blood and marrow of my soul.

I am in possession of a well maintained belly, one that has withstood the abuse and taunting of grass eating cow hugging vitamin popping aliens whose intent it seems is to die healthy, my belief is that entry into heaven will not be decided on how many push-ups or carrots I have endured, I will not be asked how many desserts I turned down or cups of dark sensual hot aromatic coffee I enjoyed either alone or in the company of friends and family.

Lesotho has reminded me that an evening playing Scrabble with a dear friend and chatting to a loved one via messaging is more meaningful than I ever imagined it to be. You may be wondering about the quote at the top of the page, well it is a picture painted with words, embellished with imagery that is so surreal you could close your eyes and picture it. My point is that we do not play enough with words, tease with them, roll them around our tongues and then set them free with a twinkle in our eye. Do not criticise another if they do not have the words in an order specified by some ancient rule still enforced and tolerated, instead embrace the fact that they are prepared to share an opinion or conversation with you. The age of electronic messaging has brought about the emergence of a new language, to deny it would be as foolish as ignoring the importance of Botox in the life of Sly Stallone, stupidity in Paris Hilton and swearing in the Kardashian household.

I have come to appreciate all communication from family, friends and loved ones in my time here, it is often the absence of something taken for granted that is seen as a pearl amidst all about us. A simple greeting and word of encouragement reminds one that they are not forgotten and still somehow needed and loved. Silence has a manner of playing havoc on the mind, almost like giving a 2-year old a fork and a bowl of peas.

I have not enjoyed being away from my special people, but have learnt so much by being forced to be alone and sharing a confined space with my demons.

Let me finish with a quote from Sore Klerkegaard, "*Life is not a problem to be solved, but a reality to be experienced*"

Nite All...

African Contracting

I have taken a brief leave of absence from composing words that stir deep emotions and sometimes anger with the occasional dose of joy; not to run off to India to hug a monk in the snow and then stare into a dirty mirror and announcing "I have found myself".

No I was simply in a rut of life overrun with frustration, sprinkled with anger and lightly dipped in anger.

Our industry of onsite engineering quality control is one where you are on the receiving end of abuse, anger and threats, yes similar to marriage except the prospect of occasional intercourse is not an option. For all purposes of logic and sanity, we are pushed to the limits of our capacity as would the mother of three year old twins, we work hard, grunt growl and flex flab and lock heads with contractors who plead innocence and sometimes beg for one more chance, just one more, Ted.

I have seen less begging and negotiating from a toddler in a toy store. It's a daily occurrence, certain conversations even begin with "How are you today Ted, you look angry". The scowl I have had surgically plastered to my frown is the same I bear when my girls use the words "yummy" and "cute" and "oooh" to describe the bottom feeding lying treacherous slimy badly clothed stealing thugs commonly referred to as teenage boys.

My work colleague Danny, a petite 148kg 6ft3 gentleman has both a tazer and a large stick which when all else fails, are his toys that he will use to escort visitors from my office. He is the gentlest of souls unless you attempt to hold his hand while he driving or insist on a man hug at any time of the day.

So why do we do it?

Its a combination of living an ex-pat lifestyle coupled with guaranteed work for a period and beats an office situation any day. The drives around site, interacting with locals and the beautiful countryside, my amazing cleaning lady who I have trained in making the perfect cuppachino are all plus factors that balance the madness.

Photographic opportunities and working alongside professionals, plus the joy of training new individuals so that they will be able to further their careers and gain valuable experience make it a joy to do what we do.

So without further ado, let me go chase off the elephants from the tree in the bush that is our urinal and until next time...

Nite All...

Willie Nelson Rocks

I like Willie Nelson.

I am sure more than half of you have clicked to the next blog by now, but hang on. If I had said I like Kim Kardashian or one of her 20 sisters then fair enough.

What makes Willie Nelson stand out for me? His hair? NO! His music? Well some of it is ok. His acting? Um I think Chuck Norris acting in a musical might do a better job. Then what is it.

He is a survivor. Born in 1933 and fighting the establishment and standing up for what he believed in has not made him a favourite with the authorities. He has ever always fought for what he believes in. In 1993 due to mismanagement of his accountants he was bankrupt and lost all he had. He started from scratch at the age of 60, me starting from scratch at the age of 43 seems like childsplay in comparison. He paid back his debts and his friends bought some of his assets and rented them back to him at a nominal rate. I too have friends that have lent me almost all that I have in my flat, I do own my own underwear and pride myself that these are replaced once they wear through in the gravity regions causing a free falling scenario I am very uncomfortable with.

He has been married 4 times and has 7 kids, he has been arrested numerous time for the possession of marijuana but I suppose we are all allowed our faults, this is what makes us human after all.

He has fought for and campaigned for many years for causes such as Farm Aid, Bio-diesel, Anti-war and animal and horse welfare.

In comparison, I advocate free speech (not hate speech) free beer (My Free the Froth Campaign is in its early stages) and encourage the "Hug Someone Daily" slogan. I have been married once and have 2 kids and have only been arrested once but not charged.

Willie Nelson is a free spirit operating within a system made to protect the middle classes from any threat to their little world they have cocooned themselves in, he fights and sings for what he believes in and has more hair on his head than I have on my entire body.

He reminds us that we need to do more than just our so-called 9-5 duty, I need to leave my comfort zone and embrace my neighbours warts and all, irrespective of their religious, social and musical choices.

Yes opera hurts but not as much as Oprah.

If they don't like beer, have a fruit juice with them.

Sundays, Cycling & Death

Sunday nights are the pits.

I am in darkest Africa and am currently camera-less, work is getting busy, but like all projects away from home the weekends are long. I am not a sociable drinker so clinging onto a bar counter like a three year old holding onto his penis is not really my thing.

My Mom and sister have knitted some teddy bears, scarves and beanies for the kids in Lesotho so this weekend they will be delivered, how my Mom manages this while looking after my Dad with advanced Parkinsons is indeed astounding. I am alone and I barely manage to look after myself, in fact if my bottom wasn't connected to my body, I am sure I would have misplaced it by now.

I have come to realise that my girls are at an age where they need their parents less and less and are becoming independant little adults. I think it is harder for a Dad to accept as they are always going to be my little angels, I mean that's why I have the chloroform, cable ties, baseball bat and hacksaw or as I prefer to call it, my "Dexter Welcoming Kit". When I am having a bad day or feeling lonely, I think of my girls or try and make contact with a friend back in SA, sometimes I find someone to chat to and sometimes they are able to chat, so I need a cuddle buddy and a chat buddy. Should you wish to apply for any of the positions, please mail me on tedlodewijks@gmail.com and I will respond accordingly, tequila or milkshakes will be supplied.

I am also considering acquiring a bicycle, my concerns are that I will be able to walk, sit or get out of the bath after my first cycle, as I am living with 15 guys I would also rather die naked in the bath than have them rescue me. So the cons by far outweigh the pros at this stage, also whoever designed cycling kit must have been more in touch with his happy side than Elton John after a couple of strawberry daquiris. And for the record guys, any drink that has an umbrella, fruit or needs to be drunk through a straw is meant for the ladies, just saying.

On that extremely biased note, I must leave you and head into a 3 hour meeting.

Nite All...

Death By Exercise

I look at a recent photo of myself and realised that I was no longer the sleek willowy athletic man I used to be.

A strict diet of beer flavored drinks and lack of vegetable based organic shakes had allowed my muscles to reach a stage of relaxation frowned upon by 99% of medical practitioners. The other 1% who performed my mammogram examination suggested the use of a sports bra. Muscle tone seemed to be less recognizable and even brief flexing in front of mirrors and at shopping centres left me feeling a little light headed. Carbo loading didn't help and neither did the intake of hops tainted energy drinks.

Sadly drastic measures needed to be taken.

Hence the migration to a mountain bike, it was found on special at a well known supermarket and looked shiny and new, wheels turned and brakes worked, surely that was all that was required? Off we went, three of us, unfit and in shorts and t-shirts, Team Disaster. Downhill was very manageable and the need for pedaling minor, I was familiarizing myself with the gearing system and determining which was front and which rear breaks. After a long and dreary 600 seconds we headed back and suddenly hit a wall of wind, severe pedaling was required and my legs were like the pistons on a formula one car, well for 2 minutes at least.

Suddenly the air thinned and I felt as if I was breathing in butane that ignited in my lungs and turned them into a crematorium at full operation, my legs began to wobble and I seemed to lose control over the amount of methane exiting my body.

It was at this point that I had to dismount occasionally and push my bike, this seemed to indicate to the locals that I wished to converse with them, the greetings and questions that were shouted at me were often followed with giggles, as I was unable to speak I nodded and attempted to ride again. With approximately 250m to go I realised that I had all my gear ratios in reverse and that was why I was pedaling like a spinning pro when gentle cycling was required.

It took an hour of lying on my bed gasping for air and not moving before I was able to remove my shoes and socks, 20 minutes of cycling had hurt me more than a Blue Bulls supporter and his team's management choice of pink camouflage rugby jerseys.

"I have been hiding from exercise, I was in the Fitness Protection Program"

Nite All...

Day 2: Hell is a Hill

Hell presented itself to me today in the form of a never ending hill, no wait, a mountain, possibly the highest in Southern Africa.

As I sweated and toiled I am convinced I could hear my FAT (Freshly Aching Tissue) collapse and fall to the ground screaming like a teenager who has been given her first credit card. I was unable to cry as this process requires tears and they come from your tear-ducts in your eyes in your head, my heart had no energy to pump blood against gravity and so my brain was dying. No brain equals no pain equals no tears, Einstein's Fictional Law of Cycles.

I was like a gazelle who gracefully fell off a cliff on the downhills and all I could hear was the flapping of my cheeks as the air filled my mouth, dodging imaginary racers and raising my buttocks to the skies in defiance. The road leveled out and rose and I was in my element, man and machine against nature. After 20m I stopped and tried to adjust the tiny screw that adjusted my gearing with my thumbnail, my nail broke and I was sure I heard the unmistakable laughter of Chuck Norris and Bear Grylls somewhere far far away. Sucking up my pride I set off again and found the local schools practicing their English with me as they overtook me on foot.

You may be asking yourself what does a pro-athlete like myself think about when they are in the zone, how the heck should I know!!!! I was wondering if it were possible to vomit up a lung and if the body would bounce if I fainted due to the altitude, after all Lesotho is not called the Mountain Kingdom for nothing. And then I looked up and I saw before me Hell, and it was bad, and I said unto myself, "Oh Crap".

I speak with with experience when I say that the road to hell is paved with tar, loose gravel and the sweat of overweight middle-aged men atoning for a lifetime of laughing in the face of exercise.

And then it was over, I crawled into a shower, lay on my bed and believe it or not planned my next ride.

Nite All...

Sunday in the Saddle

My Sunday began with a decision to head out early and tackle the road to Maseru, I left Masite Nek and as I left the cocoon of safety and fortitude of a pain-free bottom I realised that this was my first cycle on my own.

Co-rider one was asleep, grumpy and not a morning person and co-rider two decided that visiting his wife in South Africa was more important than dodging taxis on a Sunday morning. This would be my fourth ride of the week and I a step closer to emulating Lance Armstrong, I had a yellow t-shirt on, baggies, drugs in the form of blood pressure meds and happy pills and a hint of Jack Daniels in my system from the night before.

It is important that you understand that I am not some fitness freak who can hop out of bed, run 16km, cycle 24km and then pop a Berocca C and bounce through the day with a smile on my face. I could theoretically pass out if I jumped out of bed, rushing to breakfast leaves me a little flustered and jogging doesn't agree with my rugby destroyed knees or reconstructed right ankle.

I swung onto the main road, and within no time at all was being greeted my shepherds as they tended sheep, goats and cattle, in Lesotho children that are unable to attend school have the option of becoming shepherds, so its not unusual to see a 9 year old in the field tending his flock.

My admin hardened hands were taken a severe beating from the rubber grips of the handlebar, it was as if I had been entrusted with the task of removing all the skin off my palms while my backside bounced on the rocklike seat like Bo Derek bouncing assets in the running scene from the movie "10".

The Lesotho taxi-drivers are more mellowed than their South African counterparts and will hoot and give you additional space if required, this country grows on you more and more each passing month.

I am now finding that with no previous experience and not having the luxury of an experienced rider with me, it is simply a case of get on, get on with it, and get back alive. There is no plan of action, it's survive till it hurts, don't cry in front of the cheering locals and don't swear out loud. The swearing is pretty safe as I am unable to do much when gasping for air, and my throat as dry as forgotten piece of wors on a braai.

This would be my first ride where I didn't dismount and have to walk, even if it killed me. I was crawling home, with wobbly legs, collapsed lungs, bleeding hands and a huge blister of pain where my bottom was meant to be. I turned the corner and the final 200m lay before me and then it was over.

6km or 6000m lay behind me. I was a superstar!

Nite All...

Inner Peace & Screams

I used to be supple.

But that was a long time ago and when I did not have a belly that seemed to get in the way of everything and hinder my pursuit of graceful flowing stretching.

Hence I rose from my bed after charging my soul with a beer and a packet of chocolate speckled eggs and stood with my feet about a foot apart.

Gently shifting my weight from my centre to my right leg I swore as my foot immediately cramped, I moved back to my original pose and this time moved left, same result! A cramp in my left foot and the sharp pain caused me to relax to a point where an unexpected breeze escaped from my bottom. If it wasn't for the fact that I had to walk off the cramp I would have been deeply disappointed in myself.

At this moment I did not feel that I was portraying the image of a Zen master, the fact that I was clad in underpants and a Thor t-shirt and not a silk gown, along with the grunts and moans removed any air of beauty and majesty from the occasion.

I took a deep breath and tried again, this time with my arms moving like a swan shot in its wing, legs shaking and a grimace with eyes tightly closed, both feet cramped simultaneously and I tried standing on my toes as an experienced ballerina would. I simply lost my balance.

A normal man would have retired to his bed or couch and had another beer, I had neither a couch or any more beer and thus I persevered.

What followed was 3 minutes of peace and grace filled with silent screaming as my body rebelled and ached to the point where I bowed to honour the fat men who had tried and failed in a desperate attempt to find the 18 year old spirit inside their middle aged bodies.

The visions of every burger I had been enticed to devour in the name of survival floated before my eyes, every delicious silky smooth angel kissed sliver of Lindt that had been force fed to me and clutched to my hips, each cold ale that passed my lips and filled me with joy and laughter danced before me like maidens luring me with their worldly charms. My journey would require the strength of the father of a teenage daughter restraining himself from killing the smiling hormone filled potential sex offender who stood at his door asking for permission to escort his princess to a place where he would not have a clear shot at him with his sniper rifle.

My journey had just begun, and in the words of the wise man, "Have a break, have a Kit Kat", I paused and sank into my bed.

Nite All...

Permits 4 Africa

It was once again time to renew my work permit, so 10 of us trudged off to the Department of "Sit on your butt and wait Forever," and started serving our sentence.

I found myself bored after approximately 15 minutes and after another hour and a half I was photographing everything in my line of fire. I then started a game of chicken which basically involves sitting in a non-aircon room with 20 heavy breathing, hot irritated people and launching methane bombs, some stealth and others that murmured like far off thunder. I have noticed that if you pretend to be playing on your phone, keep a neutral expression and don't look up, the members of a now fully operational gas chamber have very little chance of finding the culprit.

Butt after an hour of "Spot the Bomber" I was in need of a new challenge and we were en route to the Police Station, a km walk in 32'C weather, I made friends with a lady and her friend who opened her umbrella to shield herself from the sun, I simply ducked my head under the umbrella and began chatting to her as if she was a newly found relative, she was shy, but her friend found it amusing and after a brief chat we parted ways.

Next we met a Chinese welder who had just returned from Moscow.

From his broken English we managed to derive the following information;

- Russia was very cold
- The prostitutes were very expensive
- Vodka was an essential partner in fighting off the cold
- The police were very militant and demanded to see your papers all the time.
- He had been locked up more than one
- Fucki Fucki was possible if you were not caught and bribed by the police and a lady was having a slow night

He spoke with a twinkle in his slits and a smile on his lips, he also laughed at all of us as we tried to communicate with him, a 41 year old man who still looked 30.

I was then afforded the pleasure of sharing my bench with an Indian lady, I enquired whether she sat next to me because I was handsome and irresistible to women, she giggled and blushed and looked away. My colleagues shook their heads as if they felt sorry for this poor woman.

I asked if I could have my photo taken with her and she politely declined, even when I tried to convince her that I was in fact an exotic dancer by trade and "Glitter" was my stage name. She would still not succumb to my request for a photograph. She worked with her husband for a company that manufactured all the Student Prince school shoes that were exported to South Africa, had 2 children, a son 13 and a daughter 9, she declined my offer to hold my hand while we spoke.

As I was called into the Department of "Smile and Shut Up" I was sure she was checking out my swaying bottom, but I would not put money on it.

Photo taken, permit issued and just when I felt that I had survived this 6 hour lapse in reality, we had to climb into a local taxi for a short trip, the creaking suspension, lack of windows that opened and grinding of metal on metal where brake pads should be reminded me of what the majority of commuters had to endure on a daily basis.

Africa is indeed a continent filled with colorful characters, friendly individuals and an adventure if you wish to step out of your safety net.

Be brave and live.

Nite All...

Depression

It's real, it hurts, and if not addressed it will bring you down...

New Year's Resolutions

It seems a reasonable time to bring up the matter of New Years Resolutions. We have survived January and now the real grind of work, school and life has settled into some sort of routine.

The lady in our reception at work was telling me how exhausted she is, the maddening chaos of getting back into a routine is indeed hard work and stressful. With my girls it is the parent's responsibility to buy all the text books and get them covered, stockists ran out and then the re-ordering and running up and down began.

It seems strange that my resolutions are no longer give up beer, exercise, study or save for that special unnecessary yet essential toy.

This year like last year it is simply to survive. That's it.

Times are tough and recession has hit my industry in a big way and there are times when you are unsure if you will be eating chicken or praying for an invitation to supper from a friend.

As a good friend told me, my situation is not unique and many find themselves in this predicament. The workplace has transformed itself that we very seldom are in the same field of employment that we were 10 years ago.

I have been a Coca Cola Rep, a Safety Rep, a Health Food Rep, a Travel Agent, been involved in Car Hire, worked for a national magazine and now am involved in the Quality field in Engineering and Mining. No, I didn't get paid for the exotic dancing so it's not a field of employment.

My take on Darwin is not that we originated from apes, but rather that humans evolve to adapt to and survive their present circumstances. Survival is not negotiable.

When the wheels fall off in my life and I lose hope and my sanity reaches that of Jehovah Witness at a Redneck Wedding, I call out to a very special friend. She knows me better than most and understands my chaos and somehow manages to calm me, focus my mind and encourage me.

In our darkest moments, an angel is sent to be the company we need 'til we can once again see some light.

Nite All...

Dark Chocolate World

I love dark chocolate. Slightly bitter, strong as tequila and as black as a politicians heart.

It relaxes me and helps me contemplate life, love and my spiritual journey.

I have hit a low in two of them and the recurring mantra that rocks my brain and logic is "why".

To question is natural and to doubt human. I have no superhero powers despite being able to split an apple in two with one finger, getting slapped for growling at beautiful women, and surviving two very close shaves of the unspoken kind.

I am someone who tries to wake with a smile and keep it going for as long as possible. The whole rainbow and unicorns philosophy.

Some days I succeed and then on other occasions a couple of days attack me at once and I fall quicker than Bafana Bafana head coach.

When I am in this self-preservation mode I withdraw and watch the world pass by. Waving from the shadows is like smelling a rose in your sleep. It serves no purpose and brings no joy.

Friends do that. They entertain our misery and criticism and allow us to work through it. This is what a true friend is, someone who listens and is a shoulder to lean on and in some cases a warm cup of tea or a cold beer.

Now I need dark chocolate and a dark room.

Nite All...

The Santa Session

And so it came to be that Christmas was approaching, AC/DC Christmas Rock & Roll was blasting through the Shopping Centre and the GRUMPS (Grey Rude Unhappy Miserable ParentS) were muttering under their breath about how expensive things were. They also detested the AC/DC music, after-all, the stores had been playing BoneyM and Panflute Christmas Tidings for the past 25 years, why change now! Hrmphff!

I queued for Santa with all the kids and hence drew strange looks from the parents, a little girl no older than 5 was in front of me and after staring at me for a full five minutes looked me in the eye and asked, "Where is your child"? I explained that they no longer believed in Santa and I was in the queue because I needed something from Santa. At this point her mother noticed we were chatting and moved her daughter away from me, I was given the same look Macaulay Culkin's parents first eyed Michael Jackson before vast amounts of money exchanged hands.

But did this stop the little girl, oh no. She stuck out her little hand and said, "Hello, I am Katy", I shook her hand and told her my name was Ted. Then I gave her a sweet, a sweet laden with LSD and she was hooked and died after selling her organ for drugs!!! The End!!

Well, not really. She asked why I wanted to see Santa, I told her that I needed to know what to do for Christmas, who needed a present and what did he think I should give them. She frowned a little and then looked at me and said, "A Teddy Bear or a Puppy cos no matter how scared or lonely you get, both would be there till you felt better". I thanked her and left.

You see my friends, jewellery and pretty things, even electronics age and become dated, a puppy will love you, always be happy to see you and grow with you. However, if you are unable to keep a dog, a Teddy will always be there for you no matter what. I am getting myself a Teddy for Christmas, it is my gift from Santa. Yes it is a 10 x 8cm tattoo of a battered bruised Teddy and it reminds me that despite all the trials we face, someone somewhere still needs and depends on us. Christmas is not about you, its about special family, friends and loved ones, so your obligation is to arrive and see who might need that hug or French kiss.

Nite All...

All I want for Christmas is…

What the heck do I want! I have been divorced for just over a year and have slowly carved a new life for myself.

I have a home, more than adequately kitted out. I have food, enough to throw a meal together in a jiffy should a bus load of cheerleaders come knocking on my door begging for comfort from the harsh African sun.

My net curtaining finally reaches the floor as prescribed and insisted upon by the owner of the complex, the extensions were hand cut, measured with 3 good eyes and stapled to the too short upper section. Not sophisticated perhaps, but it serves a purpose and gives me a slight moral victory!

I have coffee enough to resist the forces of tea loving visitors for a few months and spare milk hidden in case the cereal eating bunnies use all my fridge can hold.

Red wine sorted. White wine? Not necessary.

I cannot wish for world peace or to feed the starving children in Africa as this is reserved and patented by the Miss USA Association.

A cure for aids would involve the abstention of humans in the act of sex and we honestly have a better chance of Justin Bieber getting his voice back or Yoko Ono refraining from singing.

Toys I have enough of, books I have plenty that beg me to open their covers and delve into the secrets that lie within.

Love? I have the love of my girls, family and amazing friends and that will suffice me for now.

My present accommodation does not permit me to have a pet but a friend shares 2 bull terriers and allows me access time. This is more precious to me than money and makes me smile and sad at the same time. It is a true blessing.

So what is left?

What else do I require?

I know what I lust for but they are worldly things and they come and go alike.

I wish for a day of hugs, a day where smiling eyes and laughter carry me through the day and help me forget about life for a while.

That's what I want…

My Friend Monday

We all have a "special" friend, someone we have known for years, love like a brother or sister and yet are a little wary of taking them into public.

They are as loyal as an old dog and you know that if you called them at 3 in the morning to help you dispose of a body, they would. Of course you will receive a lecture next to none and a tirade of abuse as well (unless the body is that of your ex), but they would do it.

This is the same relationship I have with Mondays.

I love Monday like an old friend, we have been together as long as I can remember and have shared good and not so good memories. Monday is the puppy that licks your face at 5 in the morning wanting to play, its is also the dog poo you step in in the middle of the night.

Its the girl you loved who broke your heart and the one you will love forever but will never date.

Friday is the pop music of the week while Monday is more of the loud grunge rock you aren't quite in the mood for, its the wrong place at the wrong time.

The misfortune of being born Monday is that it has a responsibility to get you up, kick your bottom out into the street and force you to work to begin a new week. It is the bad parent who has to enforce the discipline even though it would rather play and laugh.

So, perhaps we should embrace Monday and love it a little more, thank it for always being around and knowing that no matter what, Monday will always be on our mind.

Nite All...

Meeting the Folks

The Journey to the coast and back begins with my arrival at OR Thambo International Airport. I am packed, my luggage feels heavy, laden with 15 novels for my Mom, a leatherman, cable ties, chewing gum and a torch. I am the Indiana Jones of our era, Dr Ted vs the Open Road.

I have packed a selection of music ranging from Nirvana, Sasha's Dance hits to Sherryl Crow. My underwear is sorted into casual and socialising and then driving. Have keep it all in place when you driving!

Arrived at the airport, checked in and helped an African Mama load her luggage onto the conveyor, she had one bag just for her hats and it weighed a ton!!!!!

As I entered the men's room, a gentleman smiled at me and said "Welcome to my Office". I smiled and wondered if I was meant to shake his hand? He was the cleaner who had promoted himself to MD of his department, his attitude reminded me of how far we had come as a young Democracy.

Met my cousin, took possession of the Citi Golf and after a brief stop to get some perfume for my Mom, I headed off to JBay.

Upon arrival, I walked into my parents house and met my Dad, who wasn't quite sure who I was.

He looked good, a little confused but fortunately not scared of me.

He didn't really talk to me but kept a wary eye on me. My Mom arrived and gave a kiss and Dad immediately got up and came and gave her a kiss too.

By the next morning, he walked up next to me, whacked me on the shoulder and stood next to me. It was a special moment.

The next morning he was in bed and I went in to greet him and he said "hello Ted" and gave me a kiss. That moments recognition seemed to pass quickly but was so precious.

His Parkinsons should have taken his life many years ago but his incredible stamina and my Mom's personal care and love have kept him going.

Today he walked up to me and asked me who I am, I told him I was his son, his baby. He replied that I was a bloody big baby and walked away.

There have been times when I thought I caught a glimpse of who he used to be, I cannot praise my Mom for caring for him 24/7 and refusing to give up. What a woman, what a privilege to call her my Mom and nothing I could ever do could make up for what she has done for Dad.

Rocking with Depression

I know what it feels like to be tired, moody, angry, irritable and as miserable as a Liverpool supporter, I have lived with a desire not to get out of bed in the morning and not even the allure of an exceptional cuppachino able to rouse limbs that feel hundreds of years old.

It's called depression and is basically a condition that takes the rock and roll from the soul and replaces it with Michael Bolton ballads, a fate worse than eating extra spicy curry when you have aching hemorrhoids, I am told.

My name is Ted and I am on medication for depression.

When I am on the meds, I cope perfectly well and am able to cope with most of life's curveballs, without them I am unable to process and understand and rationally deal with them at all, I am an angry teenager who cannot comprehend the need for logic as it defies my irrational tantrum. I was convinced by my therapist, doctor and friends that these were needed and the difference has been life-altering. My biggest stumbling block was "me" and seeing it as a character flaw, I was too proud initially to admit that I was not able to cope on my own, I mean just look at Batman and how happy he is! I have tried to wean myself more than once and quickly realised that they were a part of life as much as my distorted sense of humour is.

So all was going well until I discovered that I will be in Lesotho a week longer than anticipated and will be running out of my "happy I want to cuddle the world" pills. I have had to move to alternate days and with the reduction emerged my old enemy, laughing and attempting to drag me down to the cesspool from where he emerged. The battle has once more commenced.

For me to do my Mick Jagger moves with the raspiness of Bob Dylan impression, I need the little pearl of stability that comes in a white capsule and henceforth I can Rock the Depression oooooooo yeah. For now my moves are very unlike Jagger and resemble a sloth without a Garmin.

Also have the odd headache to contend with, but the light shines and the tunnel draws to a close.

Nite All...

Organised Slime

Fame and fortune and the price we have to pay for it.

If you are a female, famous and add to the qualifications above average graced with beauty, you have suddenly become the target of the paparazzi. These are the lowlifes of society that have no regard for anyone and would sell their mothers for a used cigarette butt, they waffle about in their cesspool little worlds of septic stench and taint all they come into contact with.

The sad truth is that if these festering boils of humanity had no market for their cowardly invasions of peoples privacy, they would become extinct and would hopefully cease to be and die a painful cold disease infected death.

So are they entirely to blame? No.

The publications that flaunt their wares like prostitutes invading your dining room during Sunday family lunch are as guilty for providing a livelihood for our blood sucking spineless leeches, they in turn are fed by the millions of readers who buy their filth and crave for any semi-disclosed glimpses of a breast or bottom.

We, the general public have created a monster so vile and evil that it will stop at nothing to obtain information be it true or not. They will trample on and destroy lives and families, sell their souls and trade anything for filth they can blackmail to the highest bidder.

The solution? I don't think we have one.

We live in a world were electronic data is processed and distributed quicker than the Kardashians can outswear an entire troop of marines on leave after 2 years combat.

Once the damage is done, it has very little chance of being removed from the minds of those who believe it as gospel truth.

Nite All...

Valentines Day

No I am not going mad, it is less than 3 months to Valentine's Day and in most cases for lovers young and old this far overrides the Christmas Madness.

I never used to consider the Xmas Factor as an acceptable form of referring to Christmas, but recently I have seen another side to Christmas. For family and friends and lovers is a time to celebrate, spend time together, to share, laugh and create memories to be remembered forever. It is a commercially driven holiday sold with a side dish of Christianity, the red Santa figure was created by Coca-Cola and all non-Christians hop on the ride for a free holiday.

Does this worry me? Nope

Why? Because it is a time for me to spend with my girls, reflect on a year passed and hope that I might one day spend it with someone who I love and she in turn loves me.

So am I an atheist or non-Christian?

Again no, my faith is very personal and important to me, Easter is of much more importance to me than Christmas, so I just call it as it is and celebrate it for what it is. Less guilt.

Speaking of guilt, why is it that we rely so heavily on guilt to raise kids, seek attention, enforce religion? Strange isn't it?

But back to Valentine's Day, mmmmm a real commercial success story like Xmas and Easter. Bunnies, chocolates, flowers, cards and gifts, billions spent and it supports millions of industries.

Valentines day is a happy day for most, its a day where for a week there is a buzz about as lovers scramble to find something special for their partners, my girls both teenagers have a blast and I share in their excitement as much as I can. If I am not in a relationship, hell I simply buy myself a gift and have a beer or a great glass of red wine.

So as the tunes of BoneyM and panflutes lure you to the shops, enjoy, smile and forget about that perfect figure for a while.

Happy Whatever Day my Friends

Nite All...

Easter Bunny Rocks

Now I know you have barely recovered from Christmas and for those of you in the most delightful states of togetherness, joined at the lips and hips and still munching on your Valentines Day chocolates, well brace yourselves, the Easter Bunny is coming and he wants your money.

He knows if you've been shopping
He knows when you're been good
He's gonna come a-hopping
And hide chocolate in the wood
Ooooooooooo
So get up and make some coffee
Or tea with a hot cross bun
There's so much more for you to see
This Easter's gonna be fun

I strolled into my local grocer and he had a tower of Lindt bunnies, all golden and cute and with their little bells, it is frowned upon by both my daughters and the shop attendants when I fall to my knees and laugh hysterically at the sight of Lindt, so I save my expressive artistic cravings for when I am alone.

I also aware that is a very important period in the religious sectors and I respect that, but this about the bunny.

Why a bunny?

Well its actually quite simple really and it all goes back a long long time ago.

The owl was asked by the lion who would be delivering the Easter eggs and the owl said, "Hoo, Hoo indeed".

The ostrich tried, but it got sidetracked and kept sitting on them confusing them with its own and they just melted. Then the dodo tried and this would have worked if they hadn't all run of a cliff and died. The monkeys were given a chance and they were brilliant, they climbed and scampered and got in everywhere and would have been given the job if it were not for one minor problem, they refused to give the eggs to anyone.

So what was the lion to do?

Then the owl said, "I know hoo hoo?" "Let the hare be given a chance. He is fast, has excellent hearing and eyesite, he is fast and elusive and can hide in his holes in the ground, he is the one"

And thus it came to be that the bunny came to the sole distributor of the eggs, he opened many franchises and made lots and lots of money and spent it on drugs and died. Oh hang on, that's not true.

Nite All...

Describe your God

So what don't we talk about or discuss and never question, religion.
Why?

Well we may offend someone is we had to possibly suggest that our perception of God, Jesus, Buddha or Muhammed is different to theirs, I am sure I have already offended some because their Leader of the Faith was not mentioned.

So let me start by saying that I am Christian and have been so for many years, I have had many fights with the organised church because I dare to question ideas and habits that I feel are outdated and no longer relevant in our time. This can be seen as a rebellious streak that has spanned 29 years or perhaps I am just tired of power struggles and politics that always seems to rear itself in all areas where Man needs to elevate himself.

Describe Jesus as a man and what would you say, I believe he was about 6ft tall, muscular and strong from the years of physical labour and a skin that was darkened from the days in the sun. His hands would be similar to my father-in-laws, hard and calloused with many scars from years of earning his keep as a carpenter, his hair would have been short and dark and his eyes brown. He would have been a man, someone who was as comfortable eating a meal with a bunch of fellow workers as he would have been in the presence of couples and families. He was a devout Jew and I am sure he was raised in their customs and ways.

Here is the crunch, is this what he looked like, was he tall and blond with long hair, was he black or white or something in-between? I don't care, to me it is the same as a friend of mine, I do not love them because of where they came from or what they wear or drive, I do not love them or despise them because they are beautiful or ordinary or harsh on the eye. I love them for who they are, it is something I have attempted in instill in my daughters lives and I pray it will remain with them as they mature and leave home.

Where would I find one as Jesus, would it be in an office, or a middle to upper class society? Would it be in a beautiful building or temple used for worship on a specific day of the week, I think not. The person who I believe has had the most humble yet effective life in our era was none other than Mother Theresa. She lived with those who had nothing, shared and cared and embraced a life with no luxuries and comforts, this where I would expect to find Jesus if He was around today.

My reasons for not attending church are not in the slightest pure and noble or even spiritual, they are logistical and selfish, I choose to spend the time in South Africa with my daughters and in Lesotho I have not found what I am looking for. I don't want to be a white collar Christian and attend an organisation where my 10 or 15% is required to grow that building and its administrators, I want to see it go to the folk who get their hands and knees dirty.

Rather do something once a year and embrace it than visit a club and be comfortable in a habit that clears your conscience for a week.

More than Coffee

There is a part of me that embraces the single life and single parenting because of the quality time spent with my girls, the time together is so precious that it seems to fly by quicker than a Sunday afternoon.

The fact that we can up and go and breeze into all shops and just chill is perhaps selfish at times but appreciated and adored by the three of us. We do not gladly share this time as it is ours and no we feel no guilt in saying this.

I have my flat or room to myself depending on whether I am in South Africa or Lesotho and the freedom has allowed me to ponder and philosophise about life and where it suddenly turned on me and how I managed to somehow emerge face side up. The positives is that with the help of some amazing friends, family and chemical additives I am still standing.

However, there is another side to all of this.

I live from month to month and as C so rightly informed me, so does most of the population in this country let alone the world. So what am I moaning about this time? Well, it is the reality that I am not invincible, not bullet proof and have taken a fair knock in the past 8 years, I smile, joke and tease a lot yet when I retreat into the privacy of my man cave I ponder on the future and the image I have needs some rainbows, a dawning of Aquarius and a Winnie the Pooh outlook on life. Below I have added a few that seem pertinent to me at the moment;

"Promise me you'll always remember: You're braver than you believe, and stronger than you seem, and smarter than you think."

"Weeds are flowers, too, once you get to know them."

"Good judgment comes from experience, and experience—well, that comes from poor judgment."

So, where does that leave me, well in survival mode I suppose, and yes we are allowed to have a good whinge about life and how we sometimes want to throw the towel in. The fact that I am able to rise and go to *Work Another Day* does not make me James Bond, it just makes me a single parent. Someone who, like billions of others, gets frustrated, tired and has good days and others where he just wants to get back into bed and hide under the covers.

My Simon finishes school next year and Nicole is 2 years behind, as I do what I can to prepare them for the next adventure in their lives, it has forced me to accept certain realities such as seeing less of them. Being alone and independent has created methods of coping such as hiding our true emotions from others and smiling so that you don't have to face the inevitable "Are you ok?"

So how do I conclude this essay of despair and self pity? Well, let's just say that I am not alone in it all and there are glimmers of beauty that beckon. So all in all it's one of those days where I require more than coffee.

Nite All...

Dear Karma,

I am sure you are extremely busy and as such wish to be as polite and to the point as possible.

I have some complaints for want of a better word.

1. Do you prioritise cases as they are emailed to you or is it that some are accidentally funneled into your junk folder. That sometimes happens to my mail so just want to check to see if you know about it.
2. Do requests/cases/incidents have expiry dates?
3. Just asking because you seem to be dragging your feet on some of mine. Not complaining, just mentioning it.
4. Are you harsher on repeat offenders, you see some folk have been getting so far up my nose that they have sprouted hair and are now invading my bald spot. Do repeat offenders feel your joyous wrath with more intensity?
5. Please don't tell me that there is immunity for some bottoms, because that would make for the use of language that would make Gordon Ramsay sound like the Pope.
6. Has the thought of a Karma Lotto been considered? We, the offended, get to purchase a ticket and should we win, well let's just say that you get to do what you do so well immediately.

I have spoken to some fellow colleagues who seem to share my concern that you seem to be slightly out of your depth. Have you considered roping in Santa, he is free 11 months a year and can be a real self righteous pri... um piece of work at times.

I trust I have not taken up too much of your time and await with anticipation your response or interventions.

Kids & Divorce

When we get divorced, it is not a gentle parting of two parties who no longer are able to share the same roof, it is the destruction of the family unit and all the members experience the pain and sorrow that goes along with it.

Raising Teenagers Made Simple

I will not murder them I will not murder them I will not murder them!

Sound familiar?

How many parents of teenagers have sworn this self-motivating chant to themselves?

I have 2 of the easiest most well behaved teenage daughters in the world and yet, at times I feel the urge to spice them, baste them and add the proverbial apple to the mouth and slow roast them. Remember the promise we made when we became parents and entered this world with the enthusiasm of a toddler writing on a white wall? We swore on all things holy, pure and blessed that we would NOT become like our parents. We would be different! A new generation of parenting, after all, what did our parent's know?

Reality is that we try the best we can, by trial and error, add love, frustration and worry and somehow we get through it all. I am a single Dad with enough finances to raise one and a half kids, I have two and as I ponder the expenses vs. income, I am well aware that I can not resort to exotic dancing on re-enforced tables in my sleeping hours. I no longer require beauty sleep as this is as good as it gets. The graying twitching ex-hunk is no longer able to party till 2 and bounce into the office at 7 unless he has been catapulted into his work station.

Questioning their music and in particular rappers with names like Lil Drake, 25 cents and the Usher will be the equivalent of you dancing in public in their presence.

So to those fellow parents of teenagers: we love them, we feed them and we guide them. We can do no more.

PS: in terms of shopping for clothing for these little angels, I have discovered that a fistful of cash will save you fortune in return trips exchanging items you so lovingly chose. Do not be offended, simply accept that your taste in fashion died as your eyesight deteriorated.

Nite All...

Rock and Roll Parenting

Just under a hundred miles an hour on a pothole filled road with rock and roll blaring and singing at the top of my voice.

My head is clear and I had coffee with some beautiful amazing friends this weekend. This is the mood food that your soul requires, friends, hugs, laughter and a recharging of your positive mojo.

This overflowed into my joyful singing race to the border, I was Thelma and Louise served with a side order of Chuck Norris and just a pinch of Wolverine. Do I hear a hoohah? Lol

30 days till I see my girls again so time to buckle down and work. Eat the stew, admire the scenery and stay sane. It is Nicole's birthday next week and Simon's next month. I won't be there for either, its a choice my girls and I made together when I accepted this job. I know that by seeing them 3 days a month I am missing out on a large part of their life. If I had to philosophise it all I would be as miserable as a chubby boy who can't touch his toes. Instead I smile, and when I don't, I make contact with my support crew back home.

Parenting means making tough choices; we all do and we live by them.

Bravo to every parent out there, rock and roll parenting means doing your best and smiling when you feel like crying. I admire single parents and the tenacity and inner strength they show at all times. Yes we cry behind the scenes and lie awake worrying about making it to the end of the month, we struggle to give our kids the best and beg borrow and steal to see the look of absolute joy when they have it. We are survivors and silent worriers, but dedicated and hard working and often survive by accepting love and support from our friends.

Sometimes I have to push life to the limit, it is after all rock and roll to me.

Nite All...

My Girls

I sometimes have a need to write and just clear my head of the little chaos that is currently weighing me down, I have 2 sounding boards and will reflect my thoughts and let me actually hear what I am saying.

When I have spoken to Regan or Candy, I come away with some of the mess and wandering philosophies boxed and stored in a system I am able to make sense of.

I am not the easiest person to live or work with, ask my ex-wife and I am sure she will oblige, I strive for perfection and the word "anal" has been raised on more than one occasion. I am however generous to the point of stupidity and loyal as a dog and expect nothing except a thank you in return. My latest concern has been my girls, two beautiful loving individuals who are blossoming into young ladies and have a grip on my heart so tight I could cry just thinking of them.

Simon turns sixteen shortly, she is bundle of teenage energy, master of accents and baker of note. She has the potential for greatness and I pray for her to find the right person to share this with. Show her a cookbook or the cooking channel and she will sit under her blanket and absorb and make shopping lists of "essential" ingredients as she does.

Nicole is my baby and my fighter, she wears her emotions on her sleeve and is passionate about her decisions right or wrong. She has also challenged many of my grey areas of beliefs and ideas and shattered them beyond recognition. When she decided to date across the racial line, it was time for me to reconsider my comfort zones regarding my princesses, and when my girls sat with me and discussed it and we shared our ideas I felt truly blessed to have them as my girls.

As they have grown and their independence and personalities have become more evident, I have been able to open myself to a different view and outlook on life. One should never underestimate the many ways God will reach out to us and prompt us to question what is acceptable and what needs to be challenged and perhaps thrown out if it is unfounded.

So in short, thank you my girls for your input into my life and keeping me on my toes mentally and emotionally, Daddy loves you more than you can ever imagine. Our relationship has been one of the blessings from my divorce.

Nite All...

So You Had a Crap Day…

So you had a crap day.

Its ok, no seriously it means you are normal and this is all part of the wonder experience we like to refer to as "life".

I am a two cuppachino before 09h00 in the morning person, if my schedule is somehow broken I have the potential to be as friendly as an ex-wife who cant track her maintenance payments. We all have little rituals that form part of our sanity tour and this often determines if we whistle as we work like one of those super happy little smiling dwarves or turn into the hemorrhoid man who has to cycle to work and is too scared to use the loo because of the pain.

When I reflect on the past week, month and year, I analyze the good, the bad and the ugly. I then try and understand what made me able to stabilise the bad and the ugly and what pushed me over the edge. Sometimes as I plummet into a pit of misery and depressing self pity, I am able to stop myself and recover, other times I have to swallow my pride and reach out to a friend. This reaching out is not always easy as questions will be raised that need to be answered, I don't like that because it somehow indicates that I not a superhero, merely a human.

If I now glance back over the past 3 years, I have notice that I have gone from having 1 good day a fortnight to 12. I am no longer triggered by comments and remarks from my ex and my fuse is now considerably longer. I don't question why, what and if only anymore, I have accepted what has happened and am embracing my new role as a single dad. I have also realised that being single is fine and that my job and my girls need me to be this way for a while. It will need someone who understands me and is patient to allow me to enter their lives, perhaps that person is still out there and if she isn't then that's cool as well.

As for those off days, well it's all about how we deal with them that matters. To smile and keep it all together when your steak is overcook or how you deal with a limp asparagus if you're a vegetarian tells a lot about your character.

So you had a crap day?

Nite All…

Homemade Lemonade

R6.00 for 2 lemons.

Has the world gone mad. When married I had 2 lemon trees and a lime tree in my back yard and I could never find people to take them because there were so many. According to the cost and the other ingredients required, I have decided to calculate the cost of your average glass of homemade lemonade if Sipho and Kobus were operating their BEE eLemonade Crush Stand.

The standard ratio to a simple lemonade recipe is once of water, lemon juice and sugar per serving, dissolve the sugar in some water heated on the stove and once dissolved add the balance of the ingredients and simmer.

Let it cool overnight and add fresh mint if required and serve over crushed ice.

This basic recipe is foolproof, the result is awesome and the addition of your own alcoholic derivative priceless.

The cost per glass of lemonade purchased from Sipho and Kobus will be in the region R20 per glass (just under $3). for them to make R100 each a day profit they would have to sell in the region of 40 units.

If I had to explain this to my daughters they would look me squarely in the eye and ask if I was ok. Did I really expect them to sit on a sidewalk/pavement and risk getting mugged or worse sunburnt and what would happen if their BlackBerry batteries died? Times have changed and simple is not what it used to be.

PS: I think I may make some lemonade for old times sake.

Nite All...

My Idiot's Guide to Raising Teenagers

Yes, you are the idiot. Accept it and you will be able to move on. If not, read the first sentence until it dawns on you that you are. This is not rocket science.

Somewhere between the age of 13 and nineteen, supreme insurmountable knowledge is bestowed on our angels and a level of all-knowing wisdom enters them. This will be extinguished upon them turning the ripe old age of 20 when worldly realizations of rent, work and somewhere to stay cannot be answered with mantras of "like whatever" or "just take a chill pill".

You have certain responsibilities as a parent and I will list them because like me, you do not have the capability to read and think at the same time. No, my dear fellow parent, you are not gifted.

You will work long hours, sometimes have 2 jobs to try and somehow make it to the third week of the month. You will beg, steal, borrow and refrain desperately from selling what you will consider excess body organs to keep a roof over your head, food on the table and purchase school items needed over and above school fees.

Clothing, torn costs more because it looks cool, so do not try to discuss it or refer to it as damaged or second hand, It does not matter that costs a fortune or is so cheap that the item may appear stolen, if it doesn't form part of an outfit it will be shunned, unless it is so desirable that all life on the planet will cease if it is not acquired. Are you following you me so far? Good.

This applies to the male and female teenage species and now we move onto the next item on the list, hair. We need to have access to enough products to survive a holocaust and must have both straighteners and curlers, branding is of the utmost importance because you, and I quote "can like to ruin your hair and like go bald early". Correct me if I misunderstand this, the hippies from my era had amazing hair, long and unkempt and washed infrequently, did I imagine this? When mentioned that I used to just wear a cap when I overslept and didn't have time for a shower in my youth, I feel that somehow I am about to be swallowed up by the hair gods and spat out in a hell where there are no brushes, comb, shampoo or conditioner.

The environment is "super" important, UNLESS it somehow affects our sense of dress, hair, music, food to mention a few. More deodorant is spent in one session than I use in a week and I have a neutral body odor. Oh and have I mentioned the rolling of the eyes, the hand over the eyes and shaking head and the proverbial open mouth dropped jaw looks that you will receive as a parent? They are merely expressions of amazement and hero-worship for some act that you have carried out to be remembered forever and discussed with their peers. "You are SO not gonna believe what my Dad did in the shopping centre yesterday!" See, pride and acknowledgement.

So dear parent, how do you cope with this alien that has been forced upon you?

You love it, feed and clothe it and don't attempt to understand it. We are all in need of unconditional love without judgment, however this doesn't not mean allowing them free reign over your world. By no means, your house so your rules and consequences for actions.

Nite All...

A Father's Letter

It's been a while since I put keyboard to blog and I suppose I needed an inspiration or desire to one again share what's on my heart.

This is a letter from myself to one of my daughters who is really going through a rough time and has been for a while now, I hope it will somehow put a smile on her face and let her know how much I love here even though I don't get to see her much. Perhaps it is also meant for someone else out there who feels the same way.

Hello my angel,

Firstly let me tell you that I love you, I have loved you since the first day I held you and when I think of you it makes me smile from my soul. I am battling to see the screen as I type this because, well my eyes have entered a leaking mode and I have a lump in my throat.

When you were born I never for one moment imagined what would happen to you and your sister, having to go through a divorce, changing schools, losing your home and trying to keep control of your little world as it slowly crumbled and collapsed around you. There were times when I know you cried yourself to sleep and wondered what you had done to deserve this, the answer is nothing. It was not your fault that your Mom and I parted ways, it was not your fault that you were and still are blamed for being "like your father" even though you are a thousand times the person I will ever be. You have seen so much and experienced both sides of family life, the one where it all works and the one where it's a place where you just want to scream and rage against the world, I understand when you put in your earphones and just block out the world and I understand when your eyes swell with tears as you struggle to comprehend how trust, promises and love are smashed like a red wine glass falling on a tile floor. The wine that sprays in every direction is like your heart and you try desperately to clutch and grab it to stop the pain.

What has happened to you is what is supposed to happen to other people, not you and the way it has affected your health is understandable as your system struggled to survive and recover. It doesn't make it right or fair.

When I see you sobbing as we video chat I am both overcome with sadness and at the same time love, the fact that you are able to share your pain and vulnerability as well as your joy and craziness makes me proud to be your Dad.

You have a sensitive soul and a spirit that touches peoples lives and makes them smile, when you explode into a room it's like trying to wash a wriggling puppy, everybody gets wet. You have a gift, a talent so rare that those who know you and pass through your life always remember you for your smile, laughter and compassion. So how do I fix it, well in truth I don't. I can simply walk beside you and allow you to lean on me and even carry you when it gets really bad, I can comfort you when you don't want to talk and listen when you do.

If I could simply insert a memory stick into you, download all your pain and sorrow and transfer it to myself I would, but it is a part of the amazing person you are and it has enabled you to not only grow stronger, but help so many around you.

Its never easy when those you love and trust turn on you and hurt you, its the attacks we never expect that do the most damage because we don't ever imagine it would happen.

Here is what I know;

- You are growing up into an amazing lady
- You have lots of people who appreciate you, love you and are blessed by you
- Life isn't about waiting for the storm to pass, but learning to dance in the rain
- Your capacity to love is far greater than you have ever imagined
- God loves you just the way you are because that is how He created you.

In closing, I want to thank you for helping me to see life in a different perspective, for accepting my craziness and sharing yours with me and most of all, for being who you are.

I will always love you and I miss you very much.

Dad

A Pirate Forever

If you were a pirate!

Would you, could you, hold a cutlass to the throat of a man, look him in the eye and lean and say, "Well shiver me timbers, you want to date me daughter?"

As he sweats and his lower lip trembles, would you be able to say "Is it worth losing an eye and a hand over me laddie, if ye were daft enough to attempt to kiss her or lay one of your filthy paws on her, would you hear the oncoming blade as it swings towards your ever so pale exposed neck?"

Upon the birth of daughters, there is an ancient unwritten law that permits the father to take as many lives by any means as often as he deems fit, to protect the dignity and innocence of his angels. It is also stipulated in the same creed that his daughters are never at fault and any young smelly lying heathen male who insinuates differently should be dealt a slow painful death of the father's choosing.

In days of old, it was customary for young ladies to wear chastity belts and be visible at all times.

Then there emerged the most evil of devices, the cellular phone.

It is a device so devious and despicable and when placed in the hands of a pimply overdressed hustler, allows many to hypnotise young ladies into poses and pouts no parent should ever be allowed to see. It is because of these threats that dads all over the world were solely responsible for the rise of a species called Zombies. Zombies are nothing more than teenage boys who have been injected with a Rabied Endorsed Drug Biologically Undertaking Life Loss, also commonly known as RED BULL. The state the teenager male emerges from after consumption of this drug, brainless and in seek of brains as he has none of his own, placing the entire world at risk and allows for the need of FATHER.

FATHER (Fighter Assassin Teacher Hero Eradicator Robot) is called upon to save the day, he the Bruce Willis of Destruction, the Chuck Norris of Toughness and the Incredible Hulk of Negotiators, when a teenage girl shouts "FATHER" he springs into action and protects her at all costs.

So why a pirate?

Simply because some have branded him outdated, over-protective and even, well, I hate to mention it, barbaric. Pirates served a purpose fighting for those who could not fight for themselves, they sailed seas and fought monsters and finely dressed pampered sons of the Queen to protect their treasure. Daughters are the treasure that FATHER protects and thus he is a modern day pirate, a saint whose passion is often not understood or honoured.

In closing, let this be an encouragement for all the Pirates out there, you have a mission and responsibility to uphold and protect that which is dear and sacred to you, your daughters.

Nite and happy hunting...

December Beckons

I started writing this blog under a heading entitled "Lovers" and then I basically ran out of words of the positive nature.

Why?

Well I contemplated that as we approached Christmas, it was the time that more suicides are committed than any other time of the year, so I have decided to entitle it "Surviving Christmas".

My first 2 Christmas's after my divorce were absolute hell and I longed for the day to end and for folk to leave me alone, I could see through their smiles as their eyes told me that they felt sorry for me. It was a time where was it not for my beautiful Simon and Nicole, I would have fled and just kept running.

However, friends embraced us, they welcomed us into their homes and they acted normally and didn't make a fuss over us, they allowed us to hide, blend into the shadows and withdraw when it became too much.

My 3rd Christmas was much better and I was able to interact and my girls and I smiled and joined in, we had found our niche and our reduction from 4 to 3 was now stronger than ever, bless you Brian, Dee, Zane and Trav.

Financially the past three years have been all about survival and in most cases we were not even able to give gifts, this for me was a humbling experience as I battled to receive and not return the favour. On reflection it was a time where I truly learnt more in that period of my life about grace, love, compassion and God working through people as they blessed us with gifts, love and even food. Our first Christmas together was 2 weeks after the divorce and I was so broke that homeless folk slept better than I. I had no home. A Fiat Uno with all my worldly possessions in it, and we were housesitting a friend of a friend's home. A friend took me off to Pick and Pay and bought us groceries for the holidays so that I wouldn't have to worry about feeding my girls. I will never forget that.

So this year, my wish for you and me is the same, find some friends, family or loved ones. If you have none of these then make an extra plate or two of food and drop them off with folk who would appreciate them, any old age home will have forgotten folk who will welcome sharing a cup of tea with you.

I plan to visit my folks, my Dad with advanced Parkinsons no longer remembers me and it pains me to see him in this state, but the memories are so alive and filled with love that it will be great to see him. My Mom is the rock that has and still does keep us as a family together and I have so much love and respect for her.

Don't leave it till the last minute, start your planning now and make it a Christmas to remember.

Nite All...

Miles of Smiles Part One Getting There . . .

It was a road trip that we had dreamt of, discussed and planned for months, and it was finally here.

My girls awoke me at one in the morning, we packed Daisy to the hilt and headed off to the coast, I was the designated driver and Nicole sat next me riding shotgun and keeping me awake.

Nighttime, toll roads and tarred roads as long as Granddad's tales of "when I was your age," as the road rose to meet us I found myself as relaxed as a fatboy eating a bucket of KFC and not having to share. With the sound of Sugarman humming in the background, i reflected on the past year, tough—yes, lonely—hell yes, rewarding—undoubtedly. The sacrifice that my girls and I had made when I took on my Lesotho adventure had made this holiday possible, this was the icing on the top complete with a lit candle and singing voices.

We drove and chatted and sang our lungs out, my version of white man rapping had my girls hiding their heads in shame and thus I persevered. By the time we got to Grahamstown, it was 40ºC and we were melting, no-one was singing anymore and Simon was as pale as she was red and flushed, it was as if someone had switched the cold water off in a shower we could not escape. This continued for and hour and a half and then we saw the ocean. We had arrived in JBay.

My Mom met us with hugs and a smile that I had sorely missed and I went through to see my Dad.

He was lying on his bed. He looked like a stroke victim with a huge scar on his arm when he had had a plate inserted after he had broken it. I was shocked and shaken, but put on a brave face, after all this was my Father, my hero, the man who loved and encouraged me to reach the sporting standards I had, and now he was lying here staring ahead with no recognition of me at all. My Mom came into the room and I put my arm around her and we chatted about Dad, how she managed to stay so positive through all of this will remain with me forever. The words "for better or for worse, through sickness and in health till death us do part" brought a tear to my eye and I rubbed it away quickly.

In the days ahead my Dad would improve and slowly get stronger, the Parkinsons has eaten away at him yet he fights it daily with the aid of a loving wife who refuses to give up and leave her partner of 48 years. Were it not for her, my Dad would have left us years ago.

She feeds him, washes and clothes him and changes him when he has messed himself, she talks to him throughout it all and lies with him when he sleeps. She is as protective over him as a teenager with her first cellphone.

We had arrived, tired, hot but happy.

Miles of Smiles Part Two
Beach & Shopping

Rested and fed and fed again, the girls and I headed to the beach and our first of many encounters with the surf clothing shops; Country Feeling, Billabong to name a few.

They shopped, and shopped, then shopped a little more and when I was proudly holding up a white Speedo for all to see they simply shook their heads in disbelief and shopped a little more. No, I was not permitted to try on the white Speedo and sing YMCA for the fellow shoppers, I was sent to purchase water.

R12 for a bottle of 500ml water, I asked the shop attendant if that included the Vaseline to make the whole episode less painful, the blank stare I received told me all I needed to know. I returned to my girls and ignored the security whose frail attempts to inform me that refreshments were not allowed in the shop, imagine I slipped and spilt some bottled water on a bikini or a towel, heck they would have to throw it out.

And so the shopping ended with a drunk stumbling barefooted local showing me how to reverse and then patiently waiting for payment for his expertise, we arrived at the beach. I removed my shirt and slops, flexed and relaxed my wobbly bits and with my camera round my neck followed Simon and Nicole to the waters edge. I was finally on holiday, I clicked and focused and shot everything in sight, spoke to bikini clad ladies and then photographed them, the girls were on a venture to collect shells so I photographed them as well.

The sea air, the laughter, the little kid who splashed me and whose head I was now holding under the water, it was just what I needed.

We arrived back at my parent's house and raided the fridge which was bursting as usual, went to check on my Dad and he looked much better than the previous day, the cooler weather was definitely helping. Mom and I discussed Christmas lunch which would include 3 different meats and enough food to feed a troop of JW's if they came a-knocking.

My Mom is so in control and bubbly that you would never guess that she is a pensioner/wife/nurse/cook/Mom to 4 and Granny to 3. She wakes up with a smile and just gets through the day taking all life deals her. She deals with her sorrow and hardships with a strong faith and never say die attitude.

A final trip to the shops for some last minute Christmas shopping for the girls and some more photo shooting for me and we were ready for a family Christmas. This was what the girls and I had been talking about and planning for more than 6 months, Christmas at my folks with Granny's cooking. Simon had made her now famous trifle and we fell asleep with smiles on our faces.

It was hard to believe that this was the same shattered, bruised and broken family of three that had to face Christmas three years ago, raw from divorce. Time, hard work, love and faith can indeed work miracles.

Miles of Smiles Part Three
Christmas & Beyond

I used to love Christmas, the music, tree and all its decorations, cooking for lots of people and presents and most importantly, the Christmas Service at our local Church. The second last time we attended the Service, I went dressed in my Father Christmas outfit and the looks I got from the little kids present (and some of the parents) were worth every bucket of sweat I shed in that hour.

Since the divorce, I haven't been back to a Christmas Service, perhaps next year I will pluck up the courage.

So we were ready, off to bed early, trifle made, meat ready to go into the oven, presents wrapped and Dad sleeping. The previous three year Brian, Dee and their family had opened their homes to us and we had embraced this as place of safety to survive the day. This year we wanted it to be different.

We awoke, showered, wished each other Merry Christmas and my Mom and I got my Dad out of his bed, onto the wheelchair and then into his lazyboy chair, Mom does 90% of it and I simply assist because I want to be there, its more important than life itself that I do something.

Presents on the coffee table, Simon the official distributor and me with my Canon shooting the whole event.

Lunch was amazing, my Mom feeding my Dad and the girls and I unable to move as we felt so full we were not able to lie on our bellies for fear that our heads would not reach the pillows.

It was our fourth Christmas together and finally the spirit was back again.

The next day was shell hunting (a task so dangerous that I was forced to reveal my torso to ward off the predators), a swim in the sea, and supper with Brad and Vicky. This trip had also allowed us to meet old friends, some for the first time. In an age of electronic friendships, international friendships are possible and on this trip I was determined to meet as many of my friends I had never seen face to face. Brad and Vicky are not one of those. they have a house that oozes love, food, fellowship and amazing wine. It was a home to all who entered it and no-one left empty handed.

In life there are moments where you can just feel blessed and cared for, this holiday was reaching a stage where old wounds that were sealed were being healed, it was a spiritual experience where all we encountered was love and beauty and I felt like breathing again.

The Dating Game

Room Service

Hi, I am Ted and I am divorced. Not dead, not socially outcast just divorced.

Ok so tell us Ted what the problem is? There is a problem I assume?

Well, here goes. I am a man with emotions, feelings and desires. I am attracted to beautiful women as I have been before, however before I was married and never considered an affair because of that. Now I am divorced, I do not wish to make love to every woman I see, but I would like to love and be loved.

My work circumstances do not allow for a relationship as I spend 3 days a month back in South Africa, all of which is spent with my girls.

So what, my dear friends, is a fella to do?

Rent him a lady for the pleasure of her ways and then hitch up my trousers and set off on another adventure?

Pursue the possibility of a Russian bride, limited knowledge of the English language and customs perhaps, but beautiful, loyal (I am told) and a companion.

I have agreed on principle not to mention the little people, often referred to as midgets, oh here is an advert I found on a website under "Exotic Pets".

Midget for Sale

Entertaining, friendly, clean and can be litter box trained. Perfect for leash training, fetching and tricks. Can be dressed in cute clothes.

Imagine how jealous your friends will be when they see you have your own midget.

Ok enough little side issues, back to my moral dilemma, paying a lady for her services is out of the question, the sweet Russian bride is too close to slavery in my humble opinion.

Religion degrees all activities of a sexual manner be carried out or administered within the legal restrains of marriage, sounds very erotic doesn't. "Darling, I feel a stirring and am contemplating an administration if your schedule allows it?"

So, pray do tell, what is a divorced hot blooded man to do?

Nite All...

Second Chances

You have two options in life, do it or think about it and never do anything about it.

Doing it results in yourself being open to hurt, rejected or elation and adventure. So what will you do?

I tried to play by the recognised timelines and theology that time heals all pain, and the best will be rejuvenated and possibly even superseded. I waited because initially I was incapable of giving and would have ventured into areas I had no concept of knowing how to deal with.

Let me explain.

When I first realised that I no longer loved my ex, which was about two years after the divorce, I had two huge dilemmas to overcome. The first was that I had loved her for so long after the divorce, and secondly whether I was ever able to love again. Love doesn't die overnight, it fades and slowly wilts like a flower deprived of water or a dead fish hidden under the couch of someone who did you wrong. When the realisation dawns that it is dead, you either live with the shriveled memory or you replace it with a better memory, almost like brushing your teeth after eating a Brussels' sprout covered in chocolate.

It is hard to lose faith in something, be it God, life, love or happiness and resign yourself to accepting the alternative as your new standard. God never left me, He simply needed me to stop shouting long enough to get a word in and that whisper was enough. Life means getting up no matter how difficult and soul destroying the day ahead seems and somehow facing it despite the consequences.

Love, well the harsh reality is that it may take a lot of failed dates before you find someone who will accept you as you are, you might still be looking and even reach a stage where you say "Enough".

My plea is simply to keep looking and take that chance.

Why? Because a day of smiles and laughter is worth a month of pain.

Because sunlight after a week or month of rain brings smiles and happiness.

Because you deserve better, a new chance, hope and a reason to fall asleep with a smile on your face.

Nite All...

Coffee & Sex

The origin of coffee dates back to the ninth century and what was discovered by an Ethiopian goat herder by the name of Kaldi.

The word "coffee" basically means "wine of the bean" and this addictive black magic brew has intoxicated and brought enjoyment to people all over the world. I am tempted to say that it is enjoyed more than sex and if you question this, then definitely more often than the pleasurable procreation participated in by millions.

The coffee bean was nibbled, crushed, burnt and finally boiled before it was lured into releasing its essence. It was used for medicinal purposes, aphrodisiac and taken during times of prayer before it eventually led to the first coffee shop being opened in Istanbul in the middle 1500's.

The first organised brothel however dates back to 5 BC and the Greeks are attributed with this honour.

Since then coffee shops and brothels have spread to all corners of the earth.

I must interrupt and raise a question if I may, what did people drink before Kaldi and his wandering herd of goats discovered the cocoon of caffeine. I can see the tea-drinkers bouncing up and down and clapping their hands with glee and Aunty Mildred stumbling into the room with a glass of Merlot and half its contents dribbling down her chin. Yes, yes, tea and wine have been around longer, but neither are as seductive or erotic as a roll under a duvet or a cuppachino. Sharing coffee with a friend is one of the 1.5 billion cups consumed a day, that is three times more than people making love to each other.

Just think of the different types of coffee, cuppachino, expresso, latte, mocha java, and you seem to have words so seductive that they will bring a blush to many a fair maiden.

So on that sexy note, Nite All...

Cuddling Dilemma

I am asking for opinions here and in particular from my female friends.

My question is the following, "Is it possible to have a cuddle buddy"?

It is winter and it is a time for fireplaces, red wine, Nora Jones and cuddling and chatting, it is definitely not a time to be alone unless you have two or three good books. Maybe you are a Kindle person as such are electronically bound to some me time.

I am not.

I need people and in particular do not want to be alone at the moment, I don't see the problem with a cuddle buddy, but maybe I am being selfish.

Is cuddling too intimate?

Is it only possible to cuddle with a partner that you are in a relationship, sexual or not, with or is it possible to snuggle with a friend or even a stranger?

How would a woman feel threatened if asked by a male friend to cuddle?

I have noticed that people do not seem to hug as much as they did 10 years ago, are we now moving to a society where we have less contact with humans and prefer to deal and communicate electronically? Has Apple and Blackberry killed off popping in for coffee and a chat?

So in closing, will you cuddle with me?

Nite All...

Passionate Princess

When I hear her voice I am instantly aware that passion of a woman compared to passion of a man are separated by voids not visible to the naked eye.

We all carry some underlying tone in our voices whether we are aware of it or not. Some carry a pretext of nagging, others mischievousness, cheekiness and even arrogance.

The lady in question who for purposes of this tale shall be addressed as "D" has the ability to fill a room like the faintest hint of an expensive perfume that tickles your nose as it brushes by you seductively. She giggles, flirts with her eyes as she gently bites her bottom lip and when your guard is down, has the ability to ask a question that leaves you squirming in your seat.

Picture yourself on a rooftop with a dark-haired beauty sensual in every manner sipping a delicious full-bodied glass of red wine and discussing life, love and sex. Imagine laughing and sharing as you try not to visualise the pictures you so desperately wish to for fear of falling off the roof. D is passionate about love, her children, her man and her career. When she entered politics she did so with the same energy she does life and this includes dedication, compassion and a temper so fierce I am amazed she has not entered parliament with a baseball bat.

She is as comfortable addressing a board of directors as she is serving soup at a homeless shelter with an orphan in her arms. She gives and gives and eventually crashes and burns in a heap of exhausted emotions convinced she made no difference and in these moments of human frailty, she is even more beautiful than ever. It is here that she is able to let others love and care for here and nurse her back to rock and roll political goddess mode and set her loose on our society again.

To be in the presence of a beautiful woman is indeed one of life's true blessings and when stimulated by her brain and a desire to change the world with a belief that it can be done, it inspires us to look beyond our petty emotions and focus on a larger greater need.

Nite All...

Women!!

Imagine receiving a call from a good friend in the late hours of the night and they ask you in a tense voice to come over immediately and bring with the following supplies;

- Black garbage bags
- Duct tape
- Lots of acid
- An electric saw

My immediate thought would be that a tree has fallen into his swimming pool and it needs to be sawn up, bagged and the pH-rectified in the pool, right?

Apparently not.

For the sake of this conversation lets assume that Jill called and upon arriving at the house in my lumberjack pajamas, I was informed that Jack had taken ill. She led me to the dining-room, past the patio where to my surprise I discovered that the pool was sparkling and devoid of branches, most confusing indeed. We came across Jack and I could tell he was far from well by his inability to return my greeting or acknowledge my presence, the pool of red fluid next to him was not beetroot juice and Jill's innocent glances everywhere but at me brought out the alert inner inspector in me.

More confusing was the handle of the knife protruding from between his shoulder blades, there is a slight possibility that he was peeling a stubborn beet and lost focus. What was I missing and more so, what would Sherlock Holmes do?

After a cup of coffee and a slice of chocolate cake, Jill seemed surprisingly chatty and stated that her and Jack had had words earlier and he had admitted to an extramarital affair with the babysittter. She seems to remember that he had interrupted her train of screaming and before she knew it he had stopped talking and twitching.

It was as clear as their swimming pool that she had called me over to assist her with the responsibility of choosing a new babysitter and she no longer wished to involve Jack because of his insistence to adopt a hands on approach with the hired help. I advised her as best I could and departed greeting Jack on the way out.

You may ask what can be learnt from this tale, it seems fair to assume that when a woman tells you bring over a strange array of supplies in the middle of the night, all she really wants is a friend to talk to.

Nite All...

New Love

When I first began my blogging it was a survival mechanism for keeping the demons at bay and allowing me to try and find some method in the madness and destruction of divorce. It seemed to grow and take momentum and I found that there was a certain therapeutical peace and understanding that came from sharing my darkest voyages.

This is not one of those blogs.

From the wounded soul I was able to heal and grow and most importantly accept what had happened, my girls and I found safety in a family unit of 3 and we shared in a manner I am truly blessed about.

I dabbled briefly in dating and reached a stage where I accepted that perhaps this was not meant to be for now. So I plowed my energy into my girls, friends and studying.

And then it happened.

I received an invitation for coffee from a lady I had never met. I was a little nervous and had no idea what to expect. I figured coffee was an hour at the most and then I could escape. We met, we chatted, we drank cuppachinos and I studied her without trying to get caught. Her smile reached all the way to her eyes and was as infectious as a yawn, her hands were beautiful and well manicured and she had a glow about her skin. My mouth felt a little dry and I hoped I would not open my mouth and no words would come out. I held my hands together lest she saw that I was shaking ever so slightly. It was a gloriously amazing coffee encounter.

We parted and I felt as if a part of me had left with her.

I knew that I had to see her again, I had to hold her hand and if the gods granted me one final wish, it would be to kiss her.

That was 2 months ago, her 6 year old daughter and I seemed to gel from our first meeting and my girls "approve" of the new lady in my life. I expected to lose her when my sudden departure to Lesotho appeared like a pimple on the evening of a date, I even offered her a "get out of jail free" card. Simply put, I would allow her to walk away from me with no hard feelings, fortunately she declined.

Having someone in your life that you can share with, chat to and cuddle when you can't stop smiling or crying is possibly one of life's greatest blessings. To love and be loved is beyond description.

It has been 3 years since my life crumbled to its core, but from that brokenness has arisen something so special and beautiful that it makes the journey through hell worthwhile.

Bless all of you who have encouraged, supported, cared for prayed for my girls and I. Thank you seems such an unworthy response for what it means to us.

To my two new ladies in my life, you are so much more than I ever expected or deserved.

Sad Days

Why must I leave?

I am surrounded by love and yet I must walk away and leave it behind for a month.

I don't understand this.

I had given up on love and as such had placed all relationships on hold and guess what happened, yup a lady appeared like the lady from the lake. She appraised me, digested and analysed what she had read and sat before her and decided that they added up. I was unaware that I was being "interviewed" as most guys are. Gentleman, the slightest detail, the manner in which you speak, greet her, listen and even say goodbye is checked and ticked. With most guys, the woman simply has to show up and giggle and we are sold initially.

My girls are blossoming and growing up so quickly and independently that I am seeing them in the independence and enjoying the personalities, thought processes and the manner in which they assess and judge people and situations.

Essentially they are grown-ups with a need for daddy to be around and be a bouncing board for questions when required.

I can accept that.

As for my Lisa, she makes me feel as if I can love again. I am afraid to believe it is all true because it is so real. A hug, a kiss, holding hands and sharing food, wine and thoughts together. I had accepted that this would never be again and that I was not worthy of love from another. Now that I am faced with it, I want to linger on it, savor it and somehow bottle it and take it back to Lesotho with me. It cannot be expressed in words, there are are too many senses involved.

Gabi is a 6 year old bundle of love that cuddles and giggles and has wormed her way into my heart. Bless you angel.

And yet I must leave and it hurts and tears at my emotions.

I shall return but my ladies await and I must go.

Miss you

Nite All...

Love Hurts

I wonder what caused women to begin the neverending and sometimes thankless task of pruning themselves and driving men crazy?

I mean manicures, pedicures, Botox and implants and make up that costs enough to feed a small town in outer Mongolia, and that excludes the fashion sense. Now now gentlemen, we are just as guilty and those that are not are more than likely in a long standing relationship or marriage and their partners have simply given up on them.

My journey into the Gentle Art of Beautification began when I first realised that there were creatures who lived amongst us that did not wrestle for an oblong leather ball and partake of such rituals as burping national anthems and lighting methane bursts. They were smaller, smelled different and hung around in gangs that either ignored or giggled at you. Thus began my first trip into my Dads wardrobe and I discovered the world of Old Spice and Blue Stratus, firmly believing that too much was better than too little, I could be smelt from a mile away.

My amazement was complete when I observed that not all the young ladies threw themselves at me and admired my aftershave ridden body, this I came to know as playing "Hard to Get".

But from humble beginnings I progressed to higher levels of pruning like a gaming junkie. Cut my toe nails and finger nails and didn't use them as toothpicks, had regular hair cuts and discovered shower gel.

Following my divorce, I had my first manicure and pedicure and enjoyed the relaxing pampering I received, lo and behold I found I was still straight and that these experiences had not turned me into a gay man instantly.

And then it started to get a little more intense. Nicole my daughter my 13 year old angel convinced me to shave my chest!!!!!! I did so without removing my nipples and for a week I was so itchy that I wanted to rip my shirt off and pound my naked chest like King Kong. That has now been forgotten and the hair returneth.

But was that enough? No of course not.

I heard of the term "manscaping" where one basically trims the hair down under and provides a better, less primitive attraction for purposes of this blog. I decided to approach the area concerned with a beard trimmer and with the vigor of a puppy charging a porcupine.

I gasped, hesitated and at the first sight of blood dropped the Remington butchering device and crossed my legs. This action was supposed to remove the sudden stinging pain that came from cut treasures.

DO NOT TRY THIS AT HOME!!!

The bath that followed and the 2 days of anxious walking and careful sitting was a rude reminder that some actions need to be left to professionals.

My now scarred and tender manscaped adventure has to end for now.

Nite All...

I Love Women

Why do I love women?

I have 2 amazing daughters who are my pride and joy, they radiate youth, love and a passion for life and complete our new family unity. They hug me and embrace me in their lives with all the pleasures and pressures that teenage girls are exposed to and have to deal with. Their emotions needs to be expressed and vented and as a Dad I certainly don't have the answers, one thing I have learnt from my marriage is that most times, women just want someone to listen to them, embrace then and reassure them. Its tough and tempting not to reach for the baseball bat and administer some well needed common sense to those who hurt my angels. The strength needs to be in the arms of a Dad who embraces and not one who modifies faces.

I have a Mom who has been caring for my terminally ill Dad with advanced Parkinsons for years. She doesn't complain, resists any form of assistance and on a daily basis illustrates that love can conquer all. She gives and receives so little in return; she cares and prays and continues day in and day out; laughs when I speak to her and makes me the proudest son there will ever be. How she does it? I have no idea.

I have female friends, some married and some not. They have stood by me and advise, correct and even scold me when required, they have also praised me when I least expected it and pointed out where I have changed from the man whose marriage ended rather suddenly 5 years ago. They are family to me and I know I tire them and frustrate them, yet they stay. They are beautiful and strong passionate women who reflect beauty, strength, wisdom sometimes a stubbornness I adore.

I have dated women since my divorce, wearily at first and then came to realise that most women are passionate creatures who should not be understood, but loved and spoilt. They are independent and sensual and need to converse with a man who is prepared to listen, you may glance at their sexy lumps, but sometimes a blush is required to acknowledge that you are a little shy and have a slightly higher emotional caliber than a cave man. To kiss a woman is one of life's true pleasures and seeing that slight glimmer of a smile as our lips part is a Kodak moment that is embedded in ones brain forever. I never grow tired of it.

I have contemplated long and hard on what the perfect gift is, flowers, perfume, bath salts, treats or jewelry. All have their place and time depending on the lady and as such each sends a certain message and requires a response. Lingerie delivered in a pizza box, a home cooked meal served with a glorious wine or a picnic followed with a walk holding hands all mean something different.

What do I "want" from a woman? The answer is nothing. I wish to share in their lives, their passions and roam into those areas of their minds with the assurance that I seek only to explore and delight in with their permission. I love their softness and passion as much as I admire their strength and ruthlessness.

To those that have graciously allowed me to get to know you better, thank you. You have touched me and reminded me what an honour it is to be a man, I am certainly no gentleman but have tried to be as much as I am able to.

Thank you and Nite all...

Beer Breasted Banters

I feel as I have been dragged behind Santa's sleigh since I have returned in January.

Firstly I am from Africa, I love the sun almost enough to expose my now bleached unrippled torso to it. However, I have teenage daughters who love me, but have social lives.

The days of skipping through shopping malls and pretending that I am unable to speak English seem to be over for now, I shall have to hide these superpowers until I am a grandpa and then full havoc will occur.

So what have I been doing, well I went to a beer festival in the lovely little town of Clarens in the Free State. It opened at 10 am and by 11 am I had made new friends, bought ladies in distress beer and solicited a kiss from a married woman in return for ale, I do so very much love beer. I had a Canon DSLR and spent large periods between tastings meeting people, chatting to them and taking their photos

There was the barman from Kwazulu Natal that I named Florence for his inability to produce his female assistant, he served me 3 ales and we discussed rugby, beer and why he was in fact wearing trousers when a skirt would enhance his legs so much better.

The crew from Mitchells Brewery were by far the winners and not only was their beer the best, smoothest and brought back memories of my robust post matric and army days, it was like kissing the person of your dreams, slow, gentle and sweet, growing in strength and passion until it consumes you with love and warmth as only beer can.

There was a stage where you want to hug all around you and bury your head in the ample bosoms of all the amazingly beautiful women around me, the problem was that what I saw in reality and what I saw through the camera lens led me to believe that coffee was required immediately. Yes I had already proposed to a very special lady and she was no longer talking to me.

So off to the town square and many unsuspecting characters who would be greeted, charmed and then shot Canon style. I congratulated a man who had misplaced his wife somewhere in a shop and we joked, pretended to look for her and parted laughing.

There was the coffee shop owner who was intimidated by his wife, a rare dark haired beauty who was still at the beer festival taking photos, we spoke of marriage and the role of the submissive wife in today's society, he laughed nervously and glanced over his shoulder as if he expected a beating soon.

Onto the SAB man from Cape Town with his wife and so nice to see them enjoy a cup of coffee together, these are the moments that I treasure, middle-aged teenagers talking to each other as they smile and share a special moment together.

Oh and then the noisy shop, an outlet that sold African hand-crafted musical instruments. As I approached the shop I heard noise that seemed to suggest that there were a troop of toddlers let loose and that their parents were either deaf or just exhausted, to my surprise it was an elderly couple causing all the chaos. I attempted to banish them to the naughty corner and was greeted with a look of shock, they explained that they were buying presents for their grandchildren and we laughed, I had no choice but to join them and of course photograph them.

There was the biker guy who was happy to be shot but his biker chick disapproved so he returned to his drink and would no longer speak to me, the African shopkeeper who sold me an elephant and tried to convince me to buy a camel, I don't mind camels but could never eat a whole one so I declined.

I left the town square and re-entered the beer festival, first I attempted to convince a policewoman to frisk me, her male colleagues laughed and she simply blushed and told me to go have a beer, as I have the utmost respect for the law I obliged. The costumed folk had arrived and so too the youngsters who had just surfaced from the previous evening's adventures. I bought some young men a few beers and they posed for me with smiles emulating those of lottery winners, watched a 2 man band doing a rendition of Stairway to Heaven that made me wish that my companion for the day was a lovely lady and not a 130kg friend and took some more pics as I made my way out and back to the ghost town named Bethlehem.

It was a most enjoyable and spectacular day

Moth to a Flame

A month away from home.

It contains 3 weeks of hard work and rest with exciting meals in-between added to that are weekly trips to the local cinema where we watch movies still played on a reel film system and the purring of the projector and occasional jumping of the picture.

The trip to and from Maseru is a mixture of dodging mad pedestrians who consider themselves bull bar proof and sheep who stroll in front of you as if to remind you that they are permanent residents and you are the ex-pat. To complete the trio of the "Cannonball Run" are the local vehicles. No rear lights, travelling at 50km/h in the dark on the national road and the tendency to freeze at the sight of a vehicle approaching them from the rear.

The fourth week is when it reaches the point where the chemicals are required, nerves are raw and all on Site have a tendency to growl at each other like a wife and girlfriend meeting each other for the first time, Days and hours are counted down as the weekend home looms closer and with it a list of tasks and appointments, some for necessity and some for pleasure.

And this brings me to the subject of dating, courting and flirting, and wining and dining.

My first responsibility lies with my daughters and together we anticipate the meeting after a month, a long hard hug with huge smiles and a kiss, then the next four days will be a succession of hugs and tales and holding hands as all that happened in the past month is shared and resolved if necessary.

These moments are often followed with me just watching and admiring my little ladies as they blossom into womanhood and start putting their stamp on who they will become.

I have friends that I need to see as they feed me with the positive energy and love that is so essential for my healthy mental state and positive input, these are also the creatures that know me and my devious habits and love me despite that. They share their families with me, their lives and in exceptional cases their puppies, they have become my circle of trust and those that I am accountable to.

Finally, the lady. Yes indeed, she flirts with my intellect, bedazzles me with imagery and brings a smile to my face as we discuss likes and dislikes and past and future. There is a common grasping and appreciation of food, wine, privacy and need of both intellectual and physical attractions and appreciation of family values.

I am continually intrigued on how the lack of chance applies to our lives, it serves to remind me that it is not a random rolling of the dice and many experiences and instances in our lives are moulded to bring us to where we are today. I am unique, however my circumstances are not.

The lady is a spark in a dark room and I shall continue to be drawn to her flame, perhaps this time I will not get burnt.

photo taken and used courtesy of Daniel Thorpe

Where am I now?

It has indeed been a journey of a thousand tears and ultimately a thousand smiles, by the time that this published Simon is in her second year of varsity and loving it. Nicole is about to enter Matric and her final year of schooling and I am sitting in a beautiful kitchen on a Sunday morning typing up this conclusion sipping on a cup of freshly brewed coffee.

What has happened since then?

I have returned from a three year stint in Lesotho and it took approximately 2 to 3 months to adapt to living with people again, it was a case of nowhere to hide and being surrounded by the noise, energy and availability of having it all on your doorstep versus being isolated and somewhat insulated from it all. Lesotho was hard on my family life, but good for finding out who I was and whether I could live with this new me. It was a time where I could experiment with love again, discover photography and explore new horizons. It also introduced me into the world of dating and I tried it all, well except for the "Rent a Bride" or mail order option.

I met ladies referred by friends, had picnics from hell, tried dating before and after church services (not advisable), coffee dates, encounters of the physical nature and evenings of exploration of things that go bump and ooooo in the night. Coffee dates, lunches with wine and good food and offers to meet the parents followed by demands and then insults. The good dates were on par with Willy Wonka and Hugh Heffner meeting Robin Williams in a coffee shop where Hugh supplied the waitresses, Willy the confectionaries, and Robin the entertainment. The bad however were more in line with a trip to a beauty spa with Donald Trump as your hair stylist, Ozzy Osborne your masseuse and David Hasselhoff singing the background music. Each one of these ladies left an impression on my life and for that good or bad, I am truly blessed. There were indeed drunken proposals and crying into my beer and laughing into my Jack Daniels, flirting occasions over coffee and poetry exchanged. Some bearable and others so bad it would have made Sylvester Stallone raise an eyebrow if he could.

I have since shot 3 weddings (with a camera lest you fear the inevitable), had numerous encounters of the female kind and discovered that the rules have changed, the playing field is different and men are more the hunted as opposed to the hunters. I entered the world of dating via referrals, online dating and blind dates setup by friends, it was entertaining, terrifying and exciting, however I feel that is a tale for another time and another place.

I have since met an amazing lady who burst into my life, we have moved in together. She has a daughter, 2 sons and an "adopted" daughter and our families have just grown together and accepted each other. Natalie and I continue to learn more about ourselves on a daily basis and we treasure our time together. Nats, Simon, Nicole and I have recently returned from a holiday at the coast where we visited my parents. My Mom is 71 and still cares for my Dad on her own and I am in awe of what she is capable of doing on a daily basis, she remains a pillar of strength and love and is as dedicated to my Dad as she was when they were first married 51 years ago.

My soul is content, I continue to grow and my outlook on life, religion, love and family has been transformed through the incidents and my journey through the past 6 years. Sometimes survival is enough and that is all we need to get us to a place in our lives where we are once again capable of trust, love and new beginnings. For some it happens quickly and for others it takes years and much reflection, debate and soul searching is required before we are able to move to that new chapter in our lives.

In closing, let me state the following:

> *Roses are red*
> *Violets are blue*
> *I danced with divorce*
> *And so can you*

...Before

Welcome	11
In the Beginning...	13
So the Truth,	15
Down Syndrome	17
Hello Darkness my new Fiend	19
Demons from my past	21
A Life Without Love is Not a Life	23
Midnight Heroin	25
Single.	27
Alone Tonight	29
Sanity Perhaps	31
Reflections	33
Tonight	35
Crying	37
Tonight	41
Mind Mechanics vs. Storm Running	45
Anger Management	47
Lists	49
Emotional Bouncing	51
Summons	53
The Week that was!	57
Depression	59
Today.	63
Love	65
Dating	67
Wednesday is Near	69
Subject: Divorce Care.	73
Wilderness	75
A conversation between 2 friends	75
You, Your Prostate, and Other Nasty Experiences	79
The Day Before...	81
Roses	83
16 December 2009	87
20 December 2009	91
He Offers Hope	93
25 December 2009	95
Subject: 4 January 2010	97
Fly Away	99
Hello Kim,	101
7 to 17 Jan	103
Subject: Parental Advisory Warning	105
February's Coming	107
Lesotho Nights	109
Africa Beckons	111
The African Adventure Begins	113
African Month	115
Frosty Bits	117
Rural Bathing	119
Gypsy Anyone?	121
Rent a Midget	123
Spring Fever.	125
Bullies	127
Hair Attack	129
Rock & Roll Grub.	131
The 3rd Option	133
It Approaches	135
Black and White	137
African Trimmings	139
Words	141
African Contracting	143
Willie Nelson Rocks	145
Sundays, Cycling & Death	147
Death By Exercise	149
Day 2: Hell is a Hill	151
Sunday in the Saddle	153
Inner Peace & Screams	155
Permits 4 Africa	157
Depression	161
New Year's Resolutions	163
Dark Chocolate World	165
The Santa Session	167
All I want for Christmas is....	169
My Friend Monday	171
Meeting the Folks	173
Rocking with Depression.	175
Organised Slime	177
Valentines Day	179
Easter Bunny Rocks	181
Describe your God	183
More than Coffee	185
Dear Karma,	187
Kids & Divorce	189
Raising Teenagers Made Simple	191
Rock and Roll Parenting	193
My Girls	195
So You Had a Crap Day...	197
Homemade Lemonade	199
My Idiot's Guide to Raising Teenagers	201
A Father's Letter	203
A Pirate Forever	207
December Beckons	209
Miles of Smiles Part One	
Getting There	211
Miles of Smiles Part Two	
Beach & Shopping	213
Miles of Smiles Part Three	
Christmas & Beyond	215
The Dating Game	217
Room Service	219
Second Chances	221
Coffee & Sex	223
Cuddling Dilemma	225
Passionate Princess	227
Women!!	229
New Love	231
Sad Days	233
Love Hurts	235
I Love Women	237
Beer Breasted Banters.	239
Moth to a Flame	243
Where am I now?	**245**

About Concrescent Letters

Concrescent Letters is dedicated to publishing unique works of Poetry and Prose. It takes advantage of the recent revolution in publishing technology and economics to bring forth works that, previously, might only have been circulated privately.

Now, we are growing the future together.

Colophon

This book is made of Didot and Goudy Old Style using Adobe InDesign. The cover was designed, the body was edited and set, by Sam Webster.

Except where noted, all photographs were taken by the author.

Visit our website at

Concrescent.net

www.ingramcontent.com/pod-product-compliance
Lightning Source LLC
Chambersburg PA
CBHW070556100426
42744CB00006B/307